Currency Of Conversations: The Talk You've Been Waiting For About Money

Best wishes on your financial Journey!

Lm

Linsey Mills with Andrea Stephenson

Copyright

All Rights Reserved

Copyright © 2023 Linsey Mills and Andrea Stephenson

No part of this book may be reproduced, stored in a retrieval system, or transmitted in any form or by any means, electronic, mechanical, photocopying, recording, scanning, or otherwise, except as permitted under Sections 107 or 108 of the 1976 United States Copyright Act, without the prior written permission of the author, except for brief quotations embodied in critical reviews and certain other noncommercial uses permitted by copyright law.

For permission requests, please contact CallinzGroup.com

This book is protected by copyright. Unauthorized reproduction, distribution, or use of this material without the author's permission is prohibited and may result in legal action.

Published by Callinz Group

CallinzGroup.com

Acknowledgements

Writing a book is more than a solitary endeavor; it's a symphony of collective efforts and shared wisdom. "Currency of Conversations" would not have come to life without the invaluable support, guidance, and inspiration of those who have walked this financial journey with me.

First and foremost, I extend my deepest gratitude to my sister and co-author, Andrea Stephenson. Together, we transformed countless discussions about money and finance into the pages of this book. Your dedication, organization, and unwavering commitment to this manuscript have driven its creation. I am forever thankful for the privilege of co-authoring this work with you, a true partner in every sense.

My talented wife, Michelle Serrano, has been a financial partner on this journey for more than 30 years. Your unwavering support shared financial sacrifices, and enduring commitment have been a significant part of our financial journey. From those off-campus financial workshops we attended during college to the challenges and triumphs we've faced together, you have been my steadfast companion. I am immeasurably grateful for your presence in my life.

I extend my heartfelt thanks to my clients, who have entrusted me as their financial advisor and coach for over three decades. Your stories, financial challenges, and triumphs have been invaluable lessons that have enriched my understanding of the financial world. I am immensely proud of the progress we've made together, and I cherish the trust you've placed in me. To those who have referred friends and family my way, your support has been a testament to our shared financial success, and I am profoundly grateful.

To our parents, Calvin Ray and Patricia Jean Mills, who were our first financial advisors and role models. You instilled in us the virtues of discipline, saving, homeownership, and the power of philanthropy. The principles Andrea and I have shared in this book directly reflect the timeless wisdom you imparted to us. Your legacy lives on through these pages, and I am forever indebted to you for the foundation you laid.

Writing "Currency of Conversations" has been a collaboration, learning, and reflection journey. I sincerely appreciate all who have contributed to this endeavor, whether through words, experiences, or unwavering support. This book is a testament to the power of shared knowledge, and I am honored to have had you as part of this remarkable journey.
Thanks,Linsey

Disclaimer

The content presented in this book is intended solely for informational purposes and should not be considered a substitute for professional advice. Your financial circumstances are unique, and your decisions should be based on personalized guidance from a trusted financial professional. If you have specific questions regarding your personal finances, it is advisable to seek the counsel of a qualified expert.

While this book includes stories and anecdotes drawn from the author's experiences and conversations, individuals' specific names and identifying details have been altered to protect their identities and privacy.

Our commitment is to provide valuable insights and knowledge to enhance financial literacy. To offer real-world perspectives, we will incorporate client testimonials throughout the book. In doing so, we are dedicated to upholding the utmost respect for our clients' privacy by quoting their words without disclosing personal or identifying information.

Testimonials

We wholeheartedly recommend Linsey Mills as a financial consultant and coach to anyone seeking guidance and support in their financial journey. Working with him has been an incredibly positive experience for our family, and we attribute our improved financial well-being to his expertise and personalized approach.

Linsey's extensive knowledge of personal finance combined with his exceptional coaching skills make him an invaluable asset. He has a remarkable ability to break down complex financial concepts into simple and practical steps that anyone can understand and implement. His guidance has helped us set clear financial goals and develop a strategic plan to achieve them."

One of the key strengths of Linsey is his personalized approach. He took the time to understand our unique family dynamics, financial situation, and long-term aspirations. This allowed him to tailor his advice and recommendations specifically to our needs. His dedication and genuine care for our success were evident throughout our engagement, and he consistently went above and beyond to ensure we had the tools and knowledge necessary to make informed financial decisions."

If you're considering working with Linsey as a financial consultant and coach, our advice would be to seize the opportunity without hesitation. Be prepared to be amazed by his expertise, professionalism, and unwavering commitment to your financial success. Openly discuss your goals, concerns, and challenges with him, as his ability to provide customized solutions is one of his greatest strengths.

Linsey's coaching goes beyond just managing finances; he focuses on holistic financial well-being. He not only equips you with the necessary knowledge and skills to handle your finances effectively but also instills confidence and empowers you to take control of your financial future.

—Loyal Client, 8 years

The Currency of Conversations really is the talk you've been waiting for about money! Covering everything from earning more money and budgeting to making your money work for you in a simple, easy-to-read, and interesting format, this book is filled with great information, tips, and ideas to jumpstart your journey into financial abundance and create a legacy of wealth and financial freedom for your children and future generations to come.

—Stacey K., editor

Contents

Foreword 1
Introduction 9
Section 1: Income 12
Section 2: Spending 36
Section 3: Debt 79
Section 4: Saving 105
Section 5: Investing 121
Section 6: Retirement 173
Section 7: Giving 198
Section 8: Teaching Financial Literacy to Kids 214

Foreword

What My Big Brother Taught Me about Finances by Andrea Stephenson

Linsey is eleven years older than me, so I have always looked up to him. When I was fifteen, my father died from congestive heart failure. Therefore, Linsey's role in my life became two-fold: a big brother and a father-like figure.

No matter how busy he was, Linsey always took the time to teach me something new in a fun way. I remember him incorporating games and role-play to teach me how money works. While I was in kindergarten, he taught me the value of money and how to count it.

Two years later, he moved away to college. However, the teaching continued. He and his girlfriend (now wife), Michelle, developed a program called Our-Story 101 for black children in the community. They taught children between nine and fourteen black history, financial literacy, and entrepreneurship. Because I was nine, they included me in the program. This experience allowed me to stay with my brother on a college campus for two weeks.

During my time with Our-Story 101, my cousin (who was also able to attend the program) and I started a handmade keychain business. We sold our product to family, friends, and community members. It was the first time I learned I could make something of value that people wanted. I fell in love with entrepreneurship.

After three years of facilitating this program, Linsey graduated from college and started to work as a branch manager at a bank. He and Michelle continued to find ways to teach me life skills in fun ways.

From the seventh to eleventh grade, I visited with Linsey and Michelle for two weeks each summer. They owned an award-winning T-shirt and desktop publishing business. I learned how to take orders, deliver goods to customers, budget for the company, market the product, effectively communicate, and so much more about entrepreneurship.

Additionally, through role plays, Linsey and Michelle would expose me to financial lessons like credit, debt, investing in the stock market, and mortgages. My brother gave me the book *Rich Dad Poor Dad* by Robert Kiyosaki to read. We also played Kiyosaki's game, Cash Flow, which taught me about financial sheets, liabilities, assets, income, and investing.

I remember noticing how frugal Linsey and Michelle were with their finances. They cooked most nights, drove used cars, used coupons, saved and invested their money, and didn't accumulate much debt. These lessons stayed with me during my college experience.

In college, I was a Bonner Scholar, which allowed me to get some of my tuition paid in exchange for serving the community. Bonner Scholars performed ten hours per week of community service. Many of the recipients completed community service hours through paid opportunities like being a tutor. My service hours were not paid in three out of my four college years. In my senior year, I took a paid opportunity at a school that allowed me to work with kids in an after-school program.

One of my college friends asked me how I could do community service hours without getting paid. They knew my mom was not sending me a lot of money. It was because I was frugal like Linsey and Michelle; I saved my money, only ate food in my meal plan, didn't go out a lot, and took advantage of free activities on campus. In my mind, there was nothing for me to spend money on.

After college, I went to graduate school in St. Louis and secured a studio apartment for $400 a month. I also purchased my first car in cash for $7,000, a Toyota Corolla. It was a proud moment.

I remember Linsey's concern with me taking out student loans for $40,000 for school for a master's in social work. As you know, social work is a low-paying field. Regardless, he supported my decision to attend graduate school, and I was determined to repay the loan in the future.

While in graduate school, the entrepreneurial influence from my brother and sister-in-law never left. In my spare time, I started an organization called Simply Outrageous Youth. We taught kids in the fourth through eighth grades life skills such as financial literacy and how to use Microsoft Word and Excel, and career-related skills like how to interview and write a resume.

My mentor in graduate school knew I had a passion for teaching life skills to kids, so she told me about a federal grant for after-school programs to teach enrichment subjects. I researched schools in the area that had the grant and set up appointments with their principals and vice principals.

During these meetings, I showed the principals and vice principals the curricula I had created. They were impressed. Linsey and Michelle were incredibly supportive during this time. Michelle created a template to help organize the curricula I wrote. They also sent me the materials needed to teach the classes.

I was able to secure contracts with two schools. Each school had multiple classes that needed to be taught simultaneously. Luckily, I was friends with the student community outreach coordinator, Faith, at the Masters in Business (MBA) school. I asked her for help, and she said, yes. I gave Faith copies of the curricula, and she recruited MBA students teach the classes.

This little business of mine made enough money for me to pay my rent and utilities.

After graduate school, I got a job at Entrenuity in Chicago. At the time, they were in the business of teaching kids how to start businesses. I taught many of the classes with a curriculum supplied by the company. However, I supplemented the curriculum with what I learned from Linsey and Michelle.

This job was so rewarding because these kids were making money! We had a group of boys called Chi-Town Jewelry make over $900 in sales!

After my time in Chicago, I moved to Philadelphia with money saved to establish myself as an entrepreneur. There, I used the same tactics executed in St. Louis to revamp Simply Outrageous Youth. I researched schools with federal after-school grants and made a list, and I called these schools and asked them to speak with the after-school program director.

One meeting changed my business drastically. A director gave me a list of all the federally funded after-school programs within a fifty-mile radius. After contacting the schools on this list, I had enough contracts to hire over twenty-five teachers!

Although the business was successful, I always remembered the principles taught by Michelle and Linsey to save money for a rainy day. In 2008, the rain did come because there was a significant economic downturn. Most of the schools I had contracts with lost considerable funding. As a result, I lost all my contracts except four.

I decided to get a part-time job using my master's in social work degree. It was enough to pay essential bills, save, and invest. By this time, I had met my soon-to-be husband. We decided to move to Virginia for his job. When we were looking to buy a home, Linsey told me we should live off of one income, although we were both working. My husband is great with money and has a similar financial literacy mindset as my brother.

As I write this, my husband and I have been married for over a decade and have accomplished a lot. Because of the financial lessons from Linsey and my husband being money savvy,

we live a comfortable life. By the way, the goal of paying off student loan was achieved! It is a beautiful and peaceful feeling! Like Linsey and Michelle, we cook most nights, drive used cars, shop at second-hand stores, save, invest, and strive to accumulate very little debt.

These lessons stayed with me now that I am a mom of two boys, and I have started to teach my sons these valuable money lessons. Linsey meets with my oldest over Zoom to talk about the stock market. Additionally, my oldest son visits with Linsey in the summer to learn the lessons they taught me when I was younger. I am overjoyed they are pouring this knowledge into my kids. We want to continue the legacy of living a prosperous and financially peaceful life.

How Do I Get the Most Out of This Book?

Welcome to the exciting journey to get more from your money with *Currency of Conversations*! We are so happy you've decided to invest your precious time and effort into reading our book, which we created to be engaging and conversational to make your reading experience enjoyable and enlightening.

In *Currency of Conversations*, we've taken a unique approach to presenting financial concepts by structuring the book around intriguing questions. Each question is a chapter exploring different aspects of the financial world. But don't worry, we've made sure that each chapter stands on its own, allowing you to dive right in and find the information you need without any prerequisites.

To make the book even more engaging, we've included inspiring quotes that will motivate and uplift you along the way. We are committed to providing you with invaluable insights and information to enhance your financial knowledge. In this book, we understand the importance of real-world experiences, which is why we will incorporate client testimonials throughout its chapters. To respect the privacy of our clients, we will strictly adhere to quoting their words without disclosing any personal or identifying information.

We firmly believe in the power of data visualization, so we've also incorporated graphics and charts to explain complex concepts visually.

One of the core aims of *Currency of Conversations* is to empower you to take action. We want to equip you with the knowledge and tools to make informed financial decisions. Whether you're a beginner or have some experience, this book will provide valuable insights that can shape your financial future.

Remember, you have the freedom to approach this book however you like. Feel free to jump straight to the relevant chapter if you're seeking specific information. However, if you prefer a comprehensive understanding, we encourage you to read from cover to cover. The choice is yours!

So buckle up and get ready for a captivating adventure through the fascinating world of finance. We hope that *Currency of Conversations* not only educates but also entertains you along the way. Let's embark on this journey together, one chapter at a time.

Enjoy!

Introduction

As I position my fingers on the keyboard to write the introduction to *Currency of Conversations: The Talk You've Been Waiting For About Money* I am filled with excitement and purpose. This book is not just another publication, but a culmination of years of experience, learning, and passion.

I am Linsey Mills, an investor, trader, and financial coach, and I have spent my career sharing my lessons learned about money, from the neighborhood to the boardroom. Throughout my journey, I have come to appreciate the significance of money and understand the value of saving, investing, and giving.

I often think of the analogy of a water well pump regarding money management. Just like a water well needs some water to prime the pump to get the flow started, we, too, need to have some savings and knowledge to start building wealth.

Counting my money every day was a habit I developed as a child, and it was instilled in me by my parents, who made sure that I knew the value of money and the importance of saving from a young age. As an adult, I have incorporated this habit into my morning routine of checking my financial accounts, which include bank accounts, investment accounts, cryptocurrencies, and the financial markets.

Through my passion for teaching students and interested adults about money, I have learned how to simplify complex financial concepts into easy-to-digest pieces that anyone can understand. My goal with *Currency of Conversations* is to introduce you to personal finance and investing, inspiring you to achieve your financial goals.

This book is a resource if you have ever struggled to manage your money. I understand the challenges of making sound financial decisions, especially in a world with so much information and advice. But I genuinely want readers to succeed and achieve their financial goals.

This comprehensive guide covers all aspects of money management, from budgeting and saving to investing and retirement planning. The chapters share practical tips and strategies to encourage you to make better financial decisions. The book is practical and actionable, with examples and exercises that help readers apply the concepts to their lives.

This book will help you understand the significance of financial literacy and provide you with the tools and knowledge to become financially independent. Everyone should have access to the tools and information needed to control their finances and build a promising future for themselves and their families.

Ultimately, my goal with *Currency of Conversations* is to help you achieve financial freedom. I want you to make informed decisions about your money and take control of your financial future. I want you to feel confident and empowered when managing your finances.

I am excited to share my knowledge and experiences with you through this book. It will inspire you, educate you, and empower you to take control of your financial destiny. Whether you are just starting your financial adventure or looking for ways to improve your financial health, *Currency of Conversations* is the perfect guide to help you achieve your goals.

Client Conversation: Trusted Advisor

"Finding the right financial consultant is like searching for a needle in a haystack, but I was fortunate to be referred to Linsey Mills. From the very beginning, I felt an unwavering sense of trust in him. It wasn't just a hunch; it was something I could sense in every conversation we had and I saw the sincerity in his eyes. I could tell that he genuinely cared about my financial well-being, and that made it so much easier for me to put my faith in him."

SECTION 1

Income

Like a well-nourished body, a healthy cash flow is essential for the vitality of your financial future.

~ Linsey Mills

How Do People Make Money?

When it comes to making money, there are two main ways: active income and passive income. *Active income* is the money you earn by performing specific tasks or providing services. These tasks or services are typically agreed upon by you and your employer within a certain timeframe.

Let's focus on *wages*, which is one form of active income. Wages are usually calculated based on an hourly pay rate. So the money you receive is determined by multiplying the number of hours you work by your hourly wage. It's important to note that the number of hours you work can vary weekly.

For example, let's say you earn $10 per hour, and over a two-week pay period, you work eighty hours. In this case, your gross income, which is the amount you make before any deductions or taxes, would be $800. However, if you were to fall ill and could only work forty hours within that same two-week period, your gross income for that period would be $400.

Now, some individuals earn what's known as a *salary*. This means they receive a fixed amount of money over twelve months, regardless of the number of hours they work. Usually, salaried employees are granted a specific amount of vacation and sick time for the year. Let's say you have a salary of $80,000 per year. If you take a two-week vacation and miss three days due to illness, your pay remains the same.

Moving on to another form of active income, let's talk about commissions. *Commissions* are additional earnings you receive based on the sales or deals you close. When you work on commission, the more you sell, the more money you make. Commissions can be an excellent motivator for salespeople, allowing them to benefit directly from their hard work and success.

These are just a few examples of people making money through active income. In our next discussion, we'll explore *passive income*, which involves earning money through investments, real estate, or other sources that generate income without requiring your active involvement.

How Do People on Commission Make Money?

For motivated individuals, working on commission can be exciting and rewarding. Individuals who work on a commission basis have the potential to earn more than those who receive a fixed wage or salary. When you work on commission, you earn a portion of what you sell. This means that the more products or services you successfully sell, the more money you'll make. There's a direct correlation between your sales performance and your income.

Working on commission comes with its advantages and disadvantages. On the one hand, if you're a skilled and persuasive salesperson, you have the potential to make a significant amount of money for both the company you work for and yourself. Your earnings can soar if you can close deals and generate sales. On the other hand, if you face challenges in selling the product or the market conditions are not favorable, you might find it more challenging to make enough income to cover your bills and expenses. It's important to be aware of both the potential upsides and the risks associated with commission-based work.

Choosing a product or service that people genuinely want or need is crucial to succeed in a commission-based role. Understanding your product's target market, or the type of person likely to buy it, can significantly improve your chances of making sales and boosting your earnings. This knowledge allows you to focus on reaching the right audience with the right messaging.

Regarding commission structures, there are three main types to consider. The first is *straight commission*, where 100 percent of your pay is directly tied to your sales. It's a pure-commission arrangement. The second type is *salary plus commission*, where you receive a base salary and a percentage of your sales. This provides more stability while still offering the opportunity to earn more based on your performance. Lastly, we have *graduated commission*, which means the percentage of your pay changes as you hit different sales milestones. For example, you may earn 10 percent on your first $10,000 in sales and 20 percent on the next $20,000. This type of structure provides you with an incentive to strive for higher sales numbers continuously and rewards your achievements along the way.

To sum it up, people on commission have the potential to earn a handsome income, but it requires skill, product-market fit, and a drive to excel in sales. Understanding the commission structure and choosing the right product or service to sell are vital steps toward success in this field.

Are Tips Taxable?

When it comes to tips, the US Department of Labor defines a *tipped employee* as "someone who regularly receives more than $30 per month in tips as part of their occupation." There are specific rules and regulations regarding wages and taxes for these employees.

Under federal law, tipped employees must receive a minimum cash wage of $2.13 per hour as long as the total amount they earn in tips when added to the cash wage equals or exceeds the federal minimum hourly wage. However, if the combined amount of tips and the employer's cash wage falls short of the minimum wage, the employer must make up the difference. It's important to note that many states have their own minimum wage requirements for tipped employees, which may be higher than the federal standard.

Now let's talk about the tax aspect. All cash and non-cash tips employees receive are considered income and subject to federal taxes. Cash tips given to a worker monthly are also subject to Social Security and Medicare taxes. Employees must report their cash tips to their employer, as it is required by law.

In many restaurants, a common question is whether the waitstaff actually receives the tips left by customers. The answer is yes. The employer must pay the employee the full amount of the tip indicated on a credit card transaction. If the employer keeps a portion of the tip for themselves, it is considered illegal wage theft. However, if an employee's total tips are less than $20 in a calendar month, the employee is not required to report these small amounts as income to their employer. Nonetheless, they are still obligated to report these amounts on their tax returns and pay the corresponding taxes.

In summary, tips received by employees are indeed taxable. Both employers and employees must understand and adhere to the specific wage and tax regulations related to tipped income. Both parties can avoid potential legal issues and maintain a transparent and fair compensation system by ensuring compliance with these rules.

Do Bonuses Count as Income?

Cha-ching, bonuses! These are often delightful rewards for hardworking individuals who have contributed to their company's success and met annual financial goals. When you go above and beyond, companies sometimes express their appreciation by granting you a *bonus*—a special monetary reward for your efforts.

Now, let's talk about how bonuses are treated for tax purposes. According to the Internal Revenue Service (IRS), bonuses are classified as "supplemental wages." In simpler terms, they are considered extra income separate from your regular wages. Other forms of supplemental wages may include signing bonuses or severance pay.

Some employers may attempt to provide bonuses to their employees without deducting taxes. However, this is not possible. The IRS mandates that taxes be withheld from bonus payments at the regular federal withholding rates (if the bonus is paid with regular wages) or at a flat 22 percent supplemental rate. So even though you may receive a bonus in full, a portion will be withheld for tax purposes.

You might be wondering why bonuses are subject to higher taxes. Well, since bonuses are considered "supplemental income," the IRS applies a higher tax rate to ensure they receive their fair share.

Now, one might think it would be simpler for businesses to provide salary increases instead of bonuses. However, companies often use bonuses as a means of appreciation rather than increasing salaries. This allows them to reward exceptional performance without feeling pressured to permanently raise wages across the board.

Typically, bonus percentages range between 2.5 percent and 7.5 percent of payroll. However, in some cases, bonuses can be as high as 15 percent. The specific bonus amount often depends on the company's profitability and financial performance.

To summarize, while it might be tempting for businesses to rely solely on salary increases, bonuses serve as a valuable tool for recognizing exceptional contributions and motivating employees. Bonuses are indeed considered income for tax purposes, classified as supplemental wages, and the IRS requires employers to withhold taxes on them.

How Can Businesses Make Active Income?

Businesses generate active income by actively engaging in various activities and operations. One model businesses can earn active income is through a model called *fee for service*. This concept revolves around businesses being compensated for the skills or intangible products they provide to their customers. Fee for service typically excludes things like shipping goods or interest, focusing more on the expertise and services offered. Examples of fee-for-service businesses include accounting firms, plumbing services, healthcare providers, landscaping companies, and business consulting agencies.

These businesses charge their customers based on their specialized knowledge and time invested in delivering their services. There are various ways in which businesses in this model generate revenue from their clients. For instance, a business consulting firm might charge clients hourly for their expertise. An accounting firm may opt for fixed-rate pricing, where clients pay a predetermined amount each month or per project. Healthcare providers, such as doctors, often receive reimbursements based on the number of procedures, tests, or office visits they provide.

Operating a fee-for-service business offers several advantages. First, there's no need to deal with inventory. These businesses don't have to wait for products to be manufactured or stocked before selling them. As a result, they can generate income more quickly. Individuals with specific skills can start serving customers immediately without significant lead times.

Additionally, fee-for-service businesses tend to experience higher customer retention rates, especially if they excel in customer service. Satisfied customers become loyal advocates for the business, which can lead to increased referrals and positive word-of-mouth marketing.

However, it's important to acknowledge that service-based businesses face challenges. One notable area for improvement lies in the hiring and training of service professionals. Finding reliable individuals who possess the necessary skills for the job takes time and effort. This recruitment process can temporarily impact a business's profitability. Moreover, service-based businesses are more prone to encountering dissatisfied or angry customers. Meeting and exceeding clients' expectations can be challenging, and frustrations may arise when customers demand something that cannot be fulfilled.

The most successful service businesses rely on satisfied clients to generate positive word-of-mouth marketing. They prioritize exceptional customer service, consistently going above and beyond what is expected. These businesses understand the importance of hiring quality personnel and aligning their offerings with the needs and desires of their clients.

In conclusion, businesses can earn active income through the fee-for-service model, which involves providing customers with specialized skills and intangible products. While this approach offers advantages such as quicker revenue generation and the potential for strong customer retention, it also presents challenges related to hiring and meeting client expectations. By prioritizing customer satisfaction and delivering outstanding service, businesses can thrive in the fee-for-service arena.

How Do Product-Based Businesses Work?

Product-based businesses address their clients' needs by offering tangible products that can be seen, touched, or experienced. In contrast, *service-based businesses* leverage their expertise or skills to serve their clients.

Product-based businesses can be categorized into four types: convenience goods, shopping goods, specialty goods, and unsought goods. *Convenience goods* are repeatedly purchased items, such as toothpaste or toilet paper. On the other hand, *shopping goods* are products that consumers tend to spend more time researching before making a purchase. These may include higher-end items like cars or houses. *Specialty goods* are unique and continuously strive for innovation and improvement, exemplified by products like the iPhone. Finally, *unsought goods* are products that consumers may not necessarily be enthusiastic about purchasing but do so out of necessity or for their safety. Examples of unsought goods include batteries, fire extinguishers, and life insurance.

One significant advantage of product-based businesses is their potential for scalability. Unlike with service-based businesses, their growth is not dependent on hiring more employees, expanding office space, or incurring additional overhead costs. Instead, it hinges on delivering quality products to a larger customer base. Additionally, product-based businesses often command higher valuations than their service-based counterparts, owing to their scalability and growth potential.

However, it's important to acknowledge unique challenges faced by product-based businesses. One significant hurdle is the upfront investment required. These businesses require capital for manufacturing, marketing, and product launch expenses. Once the product is created, there is no guarantee of immediate sales. While conducting market research can be helpful, it still leaves the business owner with an educated guess regarding customer demand and preferences.

Product-based businesses employ one effective strategy to generate revenue: focusing on their best-selling product. This is typically the item that produces the highest profit margins. By prioritizing and expanding on these successful products, businesses can accelerate their growth, as customers have already expressed their satisfaction and desire for more of these offerings.

Moreover, product-based businesses excel by optimizing costs to increase profitability. This involves pricing their goods at a level that consumers are willing to pay. Additionally, they leverage strategies such as bulk purchasing of raw materials, batch manufacturing to achieve economies of scale, and negotiating favorable delivery charges.

In summary, product-based businesses thrive by providing tangible solutions to their customers' needs. While they offer the advantage of scalability and often enjoy higher valuations, they also require upfront investments and face uncertainties regarding market demand. By focusing on best-selling products and optimizing costs, these businesses can increase their chances of success and profitability.

What Are Other Ways to Make Money on the Side?

Many people work their regular eight-hour shifts and assume their income potential has reached its limit. But that couldn't be further from the truth. Side hustles offer a fantastic opportunity to earn additional income alongside your full-time or part-time job. *Side hustle* refers to a job you take on in addition to your primary source of income. People pursue side hustles for various reasons, such as saving more money, paying off debt, or expanding their monthly budget.

For some, side hustles are a chance to pursue their passions. Online platforms like Fiverr or Etsy allow individuals to sell their expertise and products to people worldwide. On these platforms, people offer services like graphic design or videography or sell passion products like handmade scarves and hats. Sometimes, side hustles allow individuals to explore different types of work. For instance, a white-collar professional might be curious about trying their hand at a trade job, like plumbing, on the side.

Exciting as it may be, there are a few factors to consider before embarking on a side hustle journey. First and foremost, it's essential to remain fully engaged in your primary source of income. Side hustles should serve as additional work and income, not distractions from your primary job. To excel in your role, focus on maintaining peak performance during your primary working hours and avoid any side hustle activities. Second, ensure your side hustle doesn't interfere with your main job. If your employer discovers the overlap, it could lead to significant consequences, such as termination.

Overall, side hustles are excellent endeavors that offer opportunities to earn extra money, invest and grow your finances, explore different industries, and pursue your passions. To help you get started, here are twenty side hustle ideas:

1. Drive for Lyft or Uber.
2. Become a food delivery driver.
3. Offer your photography services.
4. Become a ghostwriter.
5. Provide grocery delivery services.
6. Engage in online tutoring.
7. Rent out your home or a spare room.
8. Resell old items from your home.
9. Offer your editing skills.
10. Babysit or pet sit.
11. Provide house cleaning services.
12. Referee youth sports events.
13. Sell handmade products online.
14. Offer music lessons.
15. Utilize your handy skills.
16. Take on freelance writing assignments.
17. Provide yardwork services.
18. Sell baked goods.
19. Engage in package delivery services.

20. Become a transcriptionist.

These are just a few ideas to inspire your side hustle journey. Remember to choose something that aligns with your interests, skills, and available time. With determination and proper planning, your side hustle can become a rewarding source of additional income and personal fulfillment.

What Is Passive Income? How about Royalties?

Passive income is a fascinating way for individuals to generate money that doesn't require continuous effort over time. Unlike *active income*, where you trade your time for money, passive income allows you to earn with minimal ongoing involvement. However, it's important to dispel the misconception that passive income doesn't require any work at all. In reality, many people invest significant effort into establishing their passive income streams initially, and once the groundwork is laid, future maintenance usually requires minimal effort. This concept is particularly applicable to earning through royalties.

Royalties are payments made to acquire the rights to use, modify, or own someone else's property, encompassing intellectual property or other creative works. The specific royalty rates are typically negotiated between the licensor and licensee based on various factors.

Numerous products and creations can generate royalties, including performing and visual arts, literary works, photographs, motion pictures, songs, music, patents, franchises, digital content, social media influencers, and even oil and gas mining. Let's explore how royalty payments work in different domains:

- Music royalties: These can be paid for the master recording, digital streaming, and downloading of musical compositions.
- Performance royalties: Payments are made for playing songs on the radio, in movies, or television shows.
- Book publishing royalties: Authors receive royalties for their copyrighted works published.

- Digital and video content royalties: Bloggers, vloggers, dancers, and music artists can earn royalties for digital and video content.
- Franchisor royalties: Franchisees pay monthly royalties to the franchisor based on a percentage of their gross sales to operate the business under the franchise's brand.
- Oil and gas royalties: Mineral rights owners receive royalties based on a percentage of the gross revenue generated from oil and gas production.
- Patent royalties: Licensees compensate patent owners for the rights to utilize their inventions per the agreement reached.

It's worth noting that US businesses can deduct royalty payments as expenses for tax purposes. Payers are required to report royalties of $10 or more paid to recipients. Passive income through royalties allows individuals to earn money from their intellectual property or creative works, so they can benefit from their creations even without active involvement. However, it's essential to understand the specific terms and agreements associated with each type of royalty payment.

Is Rental Income Good Passive Income?

Rental income can be a good source of passive income. *Rental income* is the payment received by a landlord for the use or occupation of their property, typically paid by the tenants or individuals residing in the property. Landlords use this rental income to cover housing expenses, including mortgage payments, interest, property tax, repairs, and depreciation.

Calculating rental income is relatively straightforward. It involves multiplying the monthly rent by the number of months in a year to determine the annual rental income. For example, if the monthly rent is $1,000, the annual rental income would be $12,000 ($1,000 x 12).

From a tax perspective, rental income is generally considered passive income. This means landlords or property investors typically don't need to withhold or pay payroll taxes on this income since they usually own the rental property in addition to having another job.

There are four primary ways rental payments contribute to passive income for investors: rental income itself, capital gains, tax write-offs, and debt repayment. *Rental income* from tenants serves as a source of passive income for investors. For instance, if an investor earns $12,000 per year in rental income and has $7,000 in debt payments, they would have $5,000 of passive income annually. However, it's important to note that owning rental real estate also comes with repairs, property taxes, and maintenance expenses. A property may take some time to become profitable, and many investors hold onto their properties to realize a profit over time.

They carefully choose properties in desirable locations and may gradually increase rent over time.

When investors decide to sell their rental property, they often benefit from *capital gains* if the selling price exceeds the initial purchase price. For example, if a property was purchased for $500,000 and sold six years later for $560,000, the investor would have capital gains of over $60,000. However, some landlords prefer to rely on something other than capital gains, especially if the monthly rental income already provides a profit. They aim to maintain positive cash flow from passive income for as long as possible.

Profitable rental properties are subject to taxes, which can sometimes be significant. However, various tax write-offs are available, such as depreciation and interest expense. *Depreciation* is a non-cash expense that accounts for the natural wear and tear of the property over time. Interest expense occurs when a property is financed and the annual interest on the debt can be deducted from the rental revenue when reporting taxes.

Debt repayment is another way to generate income from rental property. Rather than focusing solely on capital gains, investors consider the cash-on-cash return. For example, if a property was purchased for $500,000 and the landlord initially put down 20 percent ($100,000) over five years, the landlord may have paid down the debt to $400,000 using the rental income from tenants. It is advantageous for the landlord if the rental income exceeds the monthly debt payments, as the tenant effectively covers the principal and interest payments. The landlord can also deduct the interest expense while reducing their debt.

In summary, rental income can be a valuable source of passive income, allowing landlords to generate ongoing revenue from their properties. However, it's crucial to consider expenses, taxes, and debt management to ensure the profitability and sustainability of the rental income stream.

Can Interest Income Be Passive Income?

Interest income can be considered passive income. It refers to the money received from certain bank accounts or lending to others. There are various sources of interest income, including savings accounts, money market accounts, certificates of deposit (CDs), and corporate bonds. Let's explore each of these in more detail:

Interest on savings accounts is the amount of money banks or financial institutions pay depositors to keep their money in the bank. Banks borrow money from their account holders and lend it to other customers, paying depositors interest on their savings account balance. The interest rate paid to depositors is typically lower than the interest charged to loan customers. For example, if a customer has $1,000 in a savings account, the bank may pay them 1 percent interest, while a customer seeking a $10,000 loan may be charged 20 percent interest in addition to the principal. This is how banks generate income.

Money market accounts generally offer higher interest rates than standard savings accounts. They often provide ATM access and may allow check writing. Banks invest the deposited funds from money market accounts in regulated funds, bearing the risk on behalf of the customer. In case of any losses, the customer's account balance does not decrease.

On the other hand, money market mutual funds are uninsured investments that earn interest rates determined by inflation and Federal Reserve rates. Since these funds are invested in the market, their value can fluctuate based on market conditions.

Certificates of deposit (CDs) are low-risk savings accounts that are also FDIC insured up to $250,000, similar to savings and money market accounts. When depositing money into a CD for a fixed period, the bank pays a fixed interest rate higher than that of a savings account. Upon maturity, the customer receives their deposited amount plus any accrued interest. However, if funds are withdrawn before the CD's term ends, an early withdrawal penalty is imposed, reducing the interest earned.

Corporate bonds are debt obligations issued by companies seeking to raise capital. When you purchase a corporate bond, you lend money to the issuing corporation and receive predetermined interest payments until the bond's term expires. At maturity, the corporation repays the principal amount.

In summary, interest income can be considered passive income, which involves earning money from various interest-bearing accounts or lending arrangements. However, it's important to consider account types, risks, penalties, and market conditions when evaluating the potential passive income generated through interest.

How Do I Earn Passive Income from Dividends?

Earning passive income from dividends involves investing in stocks of companies that distribute a portion of their profits to shareholders. *Dividends* are regular payouts made by companies on a quarterly, monthly, or annual basis. Here's how you can earn passive income from dividends:

1. Understand stocks: *Stocks* represent ownership shares in a company, allowing investors to benefit from the company's growth and participate in shareholder voting rights. For instance, if a company has 100,000 shares and you own 1,000 of them, you hold a 1 percent ownership stake.

2. Dividend distribution: When a company generates profits, it can reinvest in the business or distribute dividends to its shareholders. If dividends are chosen, each shareholder receives a payment based on the number of shares they own. For example, to acquire your ownership stake, you may initially pay $10,000 (1,000 shares x $10 per share = $10,000). Then if the company you bought the stock in issues a cash dividend of $0.50 per share, you would receive $500 in dividends ($0.50 x 1,000 = $500).

3. Stock dividends: Companies can also issue *stock dividends*, where shareholders receive additional shares proportionate to their existing holdings. For instance, if the company you buy stocks in declares a 10 percent stock dividend, you would receive an additional 100 shares, resulting in 1,100 shares (10% of 1,000 is 100). This process, known as *stock dilution*, increases the total number of shares available to

investors. If the stock price rises, you can profit from having more shares than your original purchase.

To find the best dividend stocks for investment, consider the following tips:

- Look for companies with a history of paying dividends to shareholders, which can be found on the US Securities and Exchange Commission website.
- Seek companies that pay no more than 60 percent of their earnings in dividends, allocating the remaining earnings for growth.
- Analyze companies' financial reports to identify profitable businesses.
- Assess a company's income projections to gauge the likelihood of future dividend payments, aiming for around 5 percent growth over the coming years.
- Avoid businesses with excessive debt, and focus on companies with strong cash flow.
- Invest in companies operating in robust industries, as those in declining sectors may not have a sustainable future.

By investing in dividend stocks based on these considerations, you can earn passive income from regular dividend payments and benefit from the growth of your invested companies.

SECTION 2

Spending

If you are always spending a dollar here and a dollar there, you will never have enough dollars to invest and share.

~ Linsey Mills

What Are Basic Budget Needs?

Your basic budget needs are the essential expenses for your survival and well-being. These include food, rent or mortgage payments, utilities, and transportation. You must prioritize and pay these expenses, regardless of any debts or additional bills you may have. It's important to remember that taking care of yourself and your family comes first.

Let's break down these basic budget needs and discuss strategies to manage them effectively.

Food

Food is a fundamental necessity to sustain yourself and your family. According to a survey by Super Market News, Americans spend about $611 per month on groceries, including personal items. When it comes to your food budget, you have choices. You can opt for cost-effective meals centered around staples like beans and rice or enjoy more elaborate meals at home. However, frequently dining out can be expensive, as the US Bureau of

Statistics found that Americans spend an additional $329 monthly on food outside the home.

To save on food expenses, limit eating out and prioritize cooking meals at home. Additionally, consider reducing or eliminating expensive sugary drinks and opt for more affordable generic brands. The most cost-effective option is to drink water at home, and if you're concerned about tap water quality, you can invest in a water filter. Choosing dried beans and fresh vegetables over pre-packaged and pre-sliced options can also help you save, as well as buying in bulk for frequently consumed items.

Housing

Housing is typically the most significant expense for most people in the United States. In 2022, the average cost of a home was $348,079. Mortgage payments can vary, but the average monthly payment is around $2,064, excluding additional costs like homeowner insurance, home owners association fees, and maintenance expenses. Rent payments also play a significant role, with the average American paying $1,326 per month, according to a study by World Population Review.

To save on housing expenses, consider downsizing to a smaller home or finding a more affordable neighborhood, especially if your house payment exceeds 25 percent of your monthly household income. Renting out a room, getting a roommate, or exploring the option of living with family members can also help reduce housing costs. If moving is not an option, you can look for fixer-upper homes that require maintenance, as they are often available at a lower purchase price.

Utilities

Basic utilities include electricity, water, gas, sewage, and trash pick-up. Americans spend about $4,194 annually on utilities, but costs can vary based on location and usage. For instance, people in northern regions may spend more on gas and oil for heating compared to those in warmer areas.

Consider adjusting your thermostat to optimize energy usage to save on utility expenses. Setting your thermostat to 74 degrees instead of 68 degrees in the summer can result in savings. Staying hydrated with water can help you stay cool. Similarly, lowering the temperature to 69 degrees instead of 74 degrees can reduce energy consumption in the winter. Using cold water for laundry, unplugging electronic devices when not in use, and running major appliances during off-peak hours can also contribute to energy savings.

Transportation

Transportation is essential for commuting to work and purchasing groceries. While some individuals may work from home or live within walking distance of their workplace and stores, most people require transportation options.

The average American can expect to spend around $644 per month for a new car and $488 per month for an old car, not including loan interest, as many individuals finance their vehicle purchases. It's essential to consider additional costs like car insurance and maintenance.

To save on transportation expenses, using public transportation can be a significant cost-saving measure if you live in a city with reliable train, subway, or bus services. This eliminates the need for car payments, car insurance, and maintenance costs. Another option is to pay for a car with cash rather than taking out a loan, avoiding debt payments and interest charges. Purchasing a used car instead of a new one is also recommended since new cars depreciate rapidly.

Reducing trips to the gas station by carpooling, using public transportation whenever possible, planning and consolidating errands to minimize unnecessary trips can further reduce transportation expenses.

Remember, by prioritizing these basic budget needs and implementing money-saving strategies, you can effectively manage your expenses and work toward achieving financial stability.

Currency Of Conversations

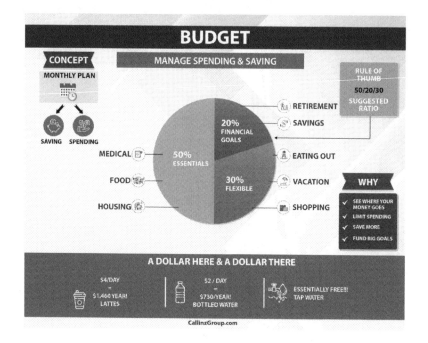

What Are Some Tips for Buying a House?

Buying a house is an exciting journey, but it can also be a lengthy process. On average, it takes about six months or even more from start to finish. Let's break it down into a few key steps to help you navigate the process:

1. Fix credit problems: If you're planning to finance your home, addressing any credit issues at least eight weeks before a lender checks your credit is essential. Check your credit report and score to see where you stand. Generally, a good credit score is required for mortgage approval. Different types of loans have additional credit score requirements. For example, a conventional loan usually requires a score of 620, while an FHA loan may be acquired with a score as low as 500.

2. Look for potential homes: Start your search online on platforms like Zillow and Redfin. These websites allow you to browse various properties and get an idea of what's available in your desired area. You can filter by the number of bedrooms, bathrooms, square footage, and other preferences. Additionally, discuss your needs and wants with your family to ensure everyone's on the same page.

3. Find a real estate agent: Working with a real estate agent is highly recommended, as they have the expertise to guide you through home buying. Take your time to research and find a reputable local agent who has experience and a good track record. Having an agent who will represent your interests exclusively during the home transition is also important.

4. Get pre-approved for a home loan: It's wise to get pre-approved for a home loan before you start house hunting. This process involves a lender verifying your income, credit, and other financial information. Pre-approval gives you a clear idea of whether you qualify for a loan and how much you can borrow. To obtain pre-approval, you must provide information about your credit history, income, assets, and debt. This process usually takes a few minutes to a couple of days, and the pre-approval is typically valid for sixty to ninety days.

4a. Manual underwriting: In some cases, you may go through a process called *manual underwriting*. This occurs when a lender manually evaluates your financial situation, such as if you have no credit history, low credit, or have experienced past financial difficulties. It's a way for lenders to assess your creditworthiness beyond traditional credit scores.

1. Find a house and make an offer: This step can take two to five months. Your real estate agent will provide you with listings that meet your requirements, but feel free to do your research as well. Once you find a home you love, your agent will help you prepare an offer to submit to the seller. The seller will then accept or reject the offer. The time it takes for an offer to be accepted can vary depending on the market conditions.

2. Closing on a home: The closing process typically takes around fifty days for a conventional purchase loan and about forty-nine days for an FHA loan. During this time, several necessary steps will take place:

- Home inspection: An inspector will evaluate the property for defects, repairs, or safety concerns.

- Appraisal: A licensed appraiser will assess the home's value to ensure it aligns with the purchase price. If the appraisal comes in lower than expected, you may need to bring more money to closing or negotiate a lower price with the seller.

- Title work: The title company will research the property's ownership history to ensure no liens or other issues. They will also issue title insurance to protect the lender against potential claims.

- Conditional approval: The lender will give conditional approval once you meet specific conditions, such as providing documentation for large withdrawals or verifying your assets.

Remember, each home-buying journey is unique, and the timeline can vary based on individual circumstances. It's essential to stay patient, work closely with your real estate agent and lender, and ask questions along the way. Good luck with your house hunting!

Currency Of Conversations

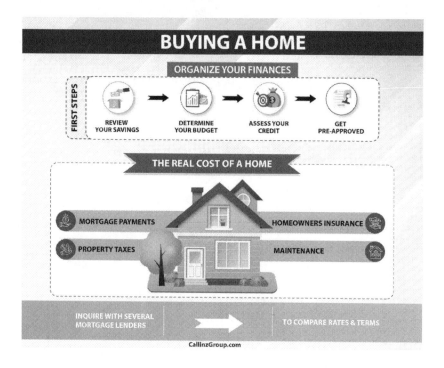

What Are the Tips for Buying a Car?

Buying a car can be a significant financial decision, so it's essential to approach it wisely. Let me share some tips to help you buy an affordable car that fits your budget:

1. Determine your car budget: Look closely at your finances and decide how much you can comfortably spend on a car. It's generally recommended to pay cash for a car instead of going into debt. If you don't have readily available funds, save a fixed monthly amount toward your car budget. Remember, the average car payment is around $500 a month, so keep that in mind.

2. Do thorough research based on your budget: Researching cars within your budget will help narrow your options. Visit local car dealer websites to see what they have available. Look for information about safety, speed, gas mileage, and comfort, and read reviews from other car owners. Websites like Kelley Blue Book can provide valuable insights into the value of different car models for a given year.

3. Get an insurance quote: Car insurance is an additional car cost. Contact your current insurance agent to get quotes for the cars on your list. Consider contacting an independent agent or getting quotes online if the price seems high. Speaking directly with an agent often helps you find better deals and more options.

4. Test drive time! Now it's time to experience the cars firsthand. Focus on test-driving cars that have features you can afford. If a dealer suggests test-driving a model with expensive upgrades, politely decline. Choose a route that

allows you to drive on the interstate and in the city to understand how the car handles different situations. Pay attention to any odd noises or delays in performance.

5. Get a car inspection: Especially for used cars, it's crucial to have a trusted mechanic perform a thorough inspection. The car may look good on the outside, but you want to ensure there are no hidden issues. If the seller hesitates to allow a car inspection, it's a red flag, and you should continue your search.

6. Buy cars at the best time: Timing can make a difference in the price you pay for a car. Consider buying at the end of the month, during holiday weekend sales, or at the end of each quarter. March, June, September, and December are good months to find deals. Going later in the day and during the week can also give you an advantage — dealerships often lower prices to meet their goals or make space for newer models.

7. Don't be afraid to negotiate: Armed with your research and the intention to pay cash, you have more negotiating power. Start by offering a lower price than you're willing to pay to leave room for compromise. Remember, walking away is okay if the seller doesn't meet your price. Always watch for other sellers offering the same car at a better price, as this can give you leverage to negotiate.

8. Leave the extras: Dealerships often try to sell you additional features and extended warranties, but these can push you over budget. You may not need a warranty if you have savings or a car maintenance fund to cover repairs. If you

want extra features later on, you can always negotiate with the dealership separately and make an informed decision instead of making impulse purchases.

I hope these tips help you in your car-buying journey. Remember to stay within your budget and make a choice that aligns with your financial goals. Happy car shopping!

Client Car Purchase Conversation:

"Linsey Mills has been my financial compass through various stages of life, helping me achieve different financial goals along the way. One such instance was when I decided to purchase a car. Linsey's expertise was on full display as he patiently walked me through the intricacies of interest rates, making sure I fully grasped their impact on my finances.

He didn't just tell me to focus on the car's price tag; he explained how interest rates, like 4% or 5%, could significantly affect the overall cost of the car over the loan term. It wasn't just about the initial $40,000 price; it was about understanding that, due to interest, I'd actually be shelling out $45,000 in total. Linsey's knack for simplifying complex financial concepts made me feel confident and informed in my decision-making."

Linsey Mills with Andrea Stephenson

What Are Tips for Paying for College?

Paying for college can be challenging, but with the right approach, you can aim to go debt-free or find ways to manage your student loans more effectively. Let's dive into some tips to help you navigate this financial journey.

1. Community college advantage: Consider starting your college journey at a community college. By doing this, you can save significant money on tuition and living expenses. Focus on taking general education or prerequisite classes that will transfer to a four-year institution later. Also explore whether your state offers free or reduced-cost college education options for high school graduates.

2. Saving money while in college: Look into on-campus work-study programs or part-time jobs. The federal work-study program can provide financial assistance based on your needs. Completing the Free Application for Federal Student Aid (FAFSA) is crucial for eligibility. Additionally, explore off-campus job opportunities in retail or sales. Another way to save money is by adjusting your meal plan if you're away from campus several days a week due to commitments like sports.

3. Finding money for college: Scholarships and grants can be a game-changer in funding your education. Treat searching for scholarships as a part-time job, and apply for as many as possible. Start with local scholarships, as they tend to have fewer applicants. Check out organizations like Kiwanis, Lion's Club, local churches, and your employer for potential scholarship opportunities. You can also explore

national scholarships, which often have more significant rewards. Look into resources like your local library, college financial aid office, high school counselor, and online databases to find relevant scholarships.

4. State-based loan repayment: Many states offer loan-forgiveness plans or loan-repayment-assistance programs. These options may require you to work in specific fields or rural areas. For instance, some states provide loan repayment assistance through a tax credit. Research if your state has programs to help with your student loans.

5. Ask your employer for help: Under the Cares Act, employers can contribute up to $5,250 toward an employee's student loans each year on a tax-advantaged basis. This benefit can be offered tax-free by the employer, providing significant relief. Some employers also offer student loan matching programs similar to 401(k) matches. Additionally, check if your employer offers access to financial advisors who can guide you in managing your loan payments alongside your other financial goals.

6. Other repayment options: Federal student loans offer various repayment plans beyond the standard ten-year repayment. Programs like Pay as You Earn (PAYE) can make monthly payments more affordable. Consider reaching out to your loan service provider to explore alternative repayment options. Adjust your lifestyle temporarily to allocate more money toward loan payments. Reducing unnecessary expenses like eating out, cable, or vacations can free up funds to pay off your loans faster.

Quick Bonus Tips:

- School choice: Unless you have a scholarship, attending an in-state public university is generally more cost-effective than a private school. Employers usually prioritize your results and experience over the specific school you attended.
- Major selection: Consider choosing a major that offers higher-paying career prospects. Fields like computer science, electrical engineering, and mechanical engineering have higher earning potential.
- Trade school options: Pay attention to the benefits of trade schools. They often have lower costs and shorter program durations and provide practical training for in-demand careers like plumbing, electrician work, or culinary arts.

Every financial situation is unique, so adapt these tips to your specific circumstances. With careful planning, resourcefulness, and a willingness to explore different options, you can make your college experience more affordable and manageable.

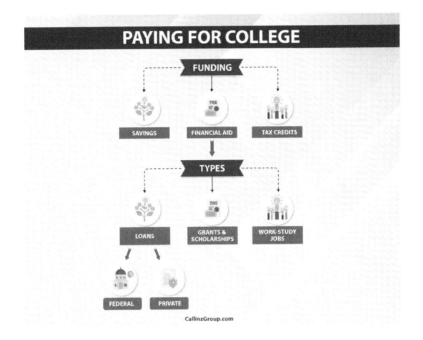

What Is the Difference Between Wants and Needs When Spending?

Understanding the difference between wants and needs when it comes to spending is crucial to managing your finances effectively. Let's break it down so it's simple to understand.

First, *needs* are the essential expenses you require for your daily living. These are the things that keep you going. They typically make up about half of your budget. Here's a basic needs list that goes beyond the bare minimum:

- Rent or mortgage payments for shelter
- Health insurance costs
- Transportation expenses (car payment, insurance, gas, etc.)
- Food
- Utilities
- Home or renter's insurance
- Child care expenses
- Job-related costs
- Simple wardrobe

There might be additional needs specific to your situation, such as legal costs like child support or past-due taxes, which are essential to prevent problems with the justice system.

On the other hand, *wants* are the things you spend money on that aren't necessary for survival. They fall under discretionary spending because they're not required for your basic needs. Some examples of wants include:

- Entertainment expenses (concerts, amusement parks, recreational activities)
- Cable TV and streaming services
- Eating out
- Travel expenses
- Most clothing (Remember, all you need is a simple wardrobe.)
- Gym memberships
- Subscriptions like apps, magazines, and other services

A well-balanced budget can include both wants and needs. However, if you're struggling to pay your essential bills or have a significant amount of consumer debt, it's essential to prioritize your needs and consider cutting back on wants. Here are a few tips to help you decrease your "want" spending:

1. Record your income and expenses: Look closely at how much you're spending each month, especially on non-essentials. It can be surprising to see how those small automatic deductions for subscription services add up over time.

2. Set a reward system: Just like we work for the reward of a paycheck, you can set spending goals with incentives attached. For example, after paying off your smallest debt, treat yourself to a small reward like dining out.

3. Remove temptations: Reduce the temptation to overspend by unsubscribing from email lists that constantly bombard you with deals and discounts. Instead, list free or low-cost

activities you can enjoy with your family, like nature trails, board games, volunteering, or backyard camping. If you're heading to a retail store, leave your credit card at home to prevent impulse purchases.

For those who aren't struggling with basic bills or excessive debt, a general rule of thumb for spending is the 50/30/20 rule. Allocate 50 percent of your budget to needs, 30 percent to wants, and 20 percent to savings. We'll delve deeper into budgeting in later discussions, but this rule is a good starting point.

Everyone's financial situation is unique, so adjust these tips to fit your circumstances. By understanding the distinction between wants and needs and making conscious choices about your spending, you'll be on your way to achieving financial stability.

How Much Do People Spend on Wants, and How Can You Save on These Items?

Let's talk about how much people typically spend on wants and how you can save on these items. It's essential to balance enjoying yourself and being mindful of your spending, and we'll show you how!

The typical American spends around $1,500 on non-essential items each year. That adds up to a whopping $18,000 annually or over a million dollars over an adult lifetime. There's nothing wrong with treating yourself occasionally, but it seems like many Americans go above and beyond. For instance, according to SwnsDigital.com, Americans spend about $20 on coffee, $209 on restaurants, and $189 on socializing with friends over drinks. There's also an average monthly expense of $108.96 on impulse purchases. Furthermore, expenses like $91 for cable, $23 for streaming services, $22 for music streaming, and $23 for additional apps contribute to the non-essential spending.

Interestingly, while people spend on these non-essential items, they often believe they can't afford essential things like saving for retirement, life insurance, car repairs, or paying off credit card debt. Many Americans could afford these essential items by adjusting their spending habits and paying less for the non-essentials.

Now, let's explore some tips on how to trim your budget and save on non-essential goods.

When it comes to entertainment expenses, there are several ways to save:

- Reduce your cable bill by cutting premium channels, or consider cutting the cable entirely and buying an antenna.
- Explore alternative ways to watch TV, like subscribing to services such as Netflix, Hulu, or YouTube.
- Lower your internet speed to reduce the monthly bill.
- Visit the local library for free to check out books, movies, TV shows, music, games, and magazines.
- Enjoy free eBooks from platforms like Kindle.
- Take advantage of nature by going outside for recreational activities.
- Have a game or movie night at home instead of going out.
- If you go to the movies, consider attending during cheaper times, like mornings or weekdays. Look out for discount days too!
- Check your city's website for free events like festivals, fairs, or concerts.

Now let's move on to saving on dining out:

- Opt for restaurants during lunchtime rather than dinner, as prices are often lower.
- Look for restaurants that offer special discounts on specific days, like "Kids Eat Free Tuesdays."
- Find restaurants that provide birthday discounts.
- Use coupons to save money on meals.
- Consider buying discounted gift cards from sites like Restaurant.com or Groupon.com.

- Have a snack before leaving home and order only an appetizer or dessert at the restaurant.
- Share a meal with someone or skip the appetizer and dessert to cut costs.
- Organize a potluck gathering at home with friends.
- Save on drinks by ordering water for free instead of buying beverages.
- Get food to go to avoid paying a tip.
- Set a budget before dining out and stick to it.
- Keep snacks in your car to prevent impulse food purchases.

Next up, let's explore how to save on subscriptions:

- Share subscription costs with someone else in your household to split the expenses.
- Consider paying for subscriptions annually instead of monthly to save money.
- Rotate your monthly subscriptions, such as using Netflix for half a year and Disney+ for the other half, instead of having multiple subscriptions at the same time.
- Research and compare prices for different subscription services.
- Downgrade to a basic plan if it still meets your needs.
- Keep track of how often you use each subscription and determine if it's worth keeping.
- Cancel any subscriptions you don't use or no longer need.

- Set reminders in your calendar to cancel subscriptions after free trial periods.
- Explore bundle services that offer multiple subscriptions at a discounted rate.

Let's move on to saving on travel:

- Pick a destination that fits within your budget.
- If traveling overseas, consider places where the American dollar stretches further.
- Research lower airfare options and consider flying on cheaper days like Tuesdays or Wednesdays.
- Explore alternative modes of transportation, such as buses or trains, instead of airplanes.
- Save on food expenses by cooking meals if you can access a kitchen, like in hostels or rented accommodations.
- Look for free walking or biking tours at your destination.
- Pack light to avoid extra baggage fees at the airport.
- Make your trip more meaningful by engaging in volunteer projects.
- Carry a reusable water bottle and refill it as you travel.
- Consider writing an eBook about your travel experiences to sell later and share valuable insights with others.

Lastly, let's discuss how to save on clothing:

- Opt for generic brands instead of expensive name-brand clothing.

- Shop off-season to get great deals on winter clothes during the summertime.
- Avoid following short-lived fashion trends and invest in classic styles that will last.
- Keep your wardrobe simple and accessorize with inexpensive items like belts, scarves, or hats.
- Utilize Google or Amazon searches to find specific items you need within a certain price range, like "men's brown boots size 10 under $35."
- Skip the dry cleaners and use your washer and dryer or home dry cleaning kits.
- Only purchase clothing items you can afford upfront rather than making monthly payments.
- Protect your clothes by folding and hanging them correctly to prolong their lifespan.
- Explore physical thrift shops, as they often offer name-brand clothes at reduced prices.
- Consider online thrift shops for convenience and a wider selection of items.
- Zip up clothes before putting them in the washer to prevent the zipper's teeth from pulling on other garments.
- Repair any clothes you own with holes or broken parts instead of immediately replacing them.
- Before buying new clothes, list three reasons you need the item to avoid impulsive purchases.

Remember, these tips are meant to guide you in making more conscious decisions about your spending. Everyone's situation is unique, so feel free to adapt these suggestions to fit your needs and preferences. By being mindful of your "wants" and finding ways to save on non-essential items, you can create a healthier financial outlook and work toward achieving your goals.

What Does Living Paycheck to Paycheck Mean? How Can You Avoid It?

Living paycheck to paycheck means that all your income goes toward paying your monthly expenses, leaving no money left over after paying bills. This common issue causes stress for many people, regardless of their income level. When living paycheck to paycheck, there is often no savings to rely on, so any unexpected expenses or emergencies can lead to depending on credit card debt, creating a cycle of financial strain.

To avoid living paycheck to paycheck, here are some tips:

1. Budget your money: Write down your income and subtract your expenses. This will help you understand where your money is going and identify areas where you can make changes.

2. Take care of the essentials first: Prioritize paying for essential expenses like housing, food, utilities, and transportation. Once these are covered, focus on other essential payments in order of importance.

3. Live below your means: Aim to live on less than you earn. This creates room for saving and investing, providing financial security and peace of mind. Living below your means also means being mindful of spending and avoiding unnecessary purchases.

4. Build an emergency fund: Start saving for unexpected expenses or emergencies by setting aside a cash reserve. Aim for a fund that covers about three to six months of your expenses. An emergency fund acts as a safety net and

reduces the need to rely on credit cards or debt in times of crisis.

5. Minimize reliance on debt: Avoid accumulating debt as much as possible. High-interest loans and credit card debt can significantly contribute to living paycheck to paycheck. Aim to pay for things in cash or use a debit card linked to your bank account.

6. Find ways to make extra money: Consider side hustles or selling items you no longer need to bring in additional income. Various opportunities are available, including remote work or selling items online through platforms like eBay or Facebook Marketplace.

7. Evaluate your budget and cut unnecessary expenses: Review your budget and identify areas where you can reduce spending. Look for non-essential items or services you can eliminate or find more cost-effective alternatives. Making small sacrifices now can lead to greater financial stability in the long run.

8. Save up for major purchases: Instead of relying on debt for significant expenses like a car or vacation, save money each month specifically for these purchases. By planning and paying in cash, you avoid paying extra interest and enjoy the peace of mind of owning these items debt-free.

9. Spend less on food: Grocery shopping can be a significant expense. Save money on groceries by checking your pantry before shopping, making a list, using store apps for deals and coupons, shopping on less crowded days for weekly

specials, buying generic brands, and comparing prices using unit prices.

Remember, the goal is to create financial stability and reduce stress. Stay focused on your objectives, celebrate your progress, and envision the financial freedom and ability to bless others that comes with smart money management.

What Are the Consequences of Debt?

Debt can have significant consequences on your financial well-being, and it's essential to understand its impact on your life. Let's dive into some disadvantages of credit card debt and discuss tips to avoid falling into credit card traps.

One of the reasons credit cards can be problematic is that they create an illusion of free money, especially for new users. Even experienced users can fall into the trap of misusing credit cards. Studies show that people spend more when using credit cards than cash. It's convenient, and you don't feel the immediate consequences of cash leaving your hand, leading to higher spending habits.

Interest plays a significant role in making credit card balances challenging to pay off. Approximately 45 percent of Americans manage to avoid interest by paying off their balances monthly. However, for many, a portion of their payments goes toward interest, prolonging the time it takes to become debt-free.

Another issue is that people often don't stop at one credit card. They continue borrowing money, which deepens their debt and hinders progress toward other financial goals, such as saving for retirement or going on a dream vacation. Accumulating debt restricts monthly cash flow, leaving individuals feeling trapped in jobs they may not enjoy.

The stress caused by mounting debt can take a toll on both physical and mental health, leading to a high-stress situation that affects overall well-being. Credit cards also have a significant impact on your credit score. Consistently paying bills on time each month helps maintain a good credit score. However, a single mistake, like missing a payment, can drop your score. Repeated mistakes will lead to a significant decline in your creditworthiness.

Making minimum payments on credit cards might help you avoid late fees, but there are better strategies for paying off your balance. You'll spend more time paying off the balance and accruing interest by making only minimum payments. It's important to understand that a $7,000 credit balance can balloon to $200,000 if you only make minimum payments for thirty years.

Tracking your spending is crucial for financial management. However, having multiple credit cards and cash and debit cards makes it challenging to track where your money is going. This can lead to overspending and financial mismanagement.

To use credit cards responsibly, here are some quick tips. However, if you lack the discipline to stick to a plan, it's best to use cash or a debit card:

- Set a spending limit on your credit card within your budget and below the credit limit.
- Don't use credit cards to live a lifestyle you can't afford or to impress others.
- Pay your balance in full each month to avoid interest charges. If you can't afford to do so, you are likely charging more than you can afford.
- If you can't pay the balance in full, pay as much as possible, preferably above the minimum payment, to reduce the balance and the amount of interest paid.
- If you find it challenging to pay off the balance, stop using credit cards and focus on living within your means.

- Keep your credit card balances at 30 percent or less of your credit limit.
- Always contact your credit card company to understand the terms and interest rates clearly.
- Track your spending using finance software or simply pen and paper.
- Regularly monitor your credit card activity and report any suspicious transactions promptly.

Understanding the consequences of debt and utilizing credit cards responsibly can help you avoid financial pitfalls and work toward a more secure financial future.

Linsey Mills with Andrea Stephenson

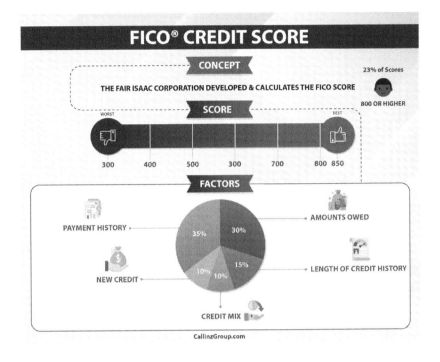

Why Are Taxes Needed?

Taxes are essential to how our government operates and provide various services and resources that benefit our society. We pay taxes to support entities, projects, and activities such as libraries, schools, roads, parks, hospitals, the military, police, fire departments, and more. The United States has the Internal Revenue Service (IRS), which is responsible for collecting taxes and enforcing tax laws.

There are different types of taxes that we encounter:

- *Income tax* is a tax on the money individuals or businesses earn. The amount you pay depends on how much you make in a year. Income taxes are collected at the federal level and sometimes at the state and local levels.
- *Corporate tax* is based on a company's earnings after deducting all expenses.
- *Payroll taxes* are collected from employee wages and salaries by employers, both on the federal and state levels.
- *Sales tax* is levied on the money people spend. A fixed percentage is applied to each sale and is typically collected at the state and local levels.
- *Property tax* is a home, land, or commercial real estate tax. It is an additional cost for property owners.
- *Capital gains* tax is paid on the growth or profit from an investment when it is sold.

The due date for federal and state income taxes is usually April 15. However, the deadline may be moved if this day falls on a holiday or weekend. Giving yourself enough time to prepare your taxes before the due date is important. If you can't complete your taxes by April 15, you can apply for a free extension, which typically gives you until October to file.

If you fail to pay your taxes, the IRS will contact you. They have alternative methods to collect taxes, such as placing holds on your bank accounts, wage garnishments, or property liens. Property liens can hurt your credit score. The only way to stop liens is to pay the tax balance in full.

The complexity of taxes can vary depending on your situation. In this book, we will delve into more detail on this topic. The following section will discuss whether you should handle your taxes or seek professional assistance.

Currency Of Conversations

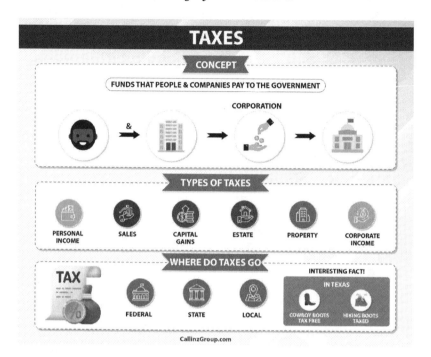

Should I File My Own Taxes?

When it comes to filing your taxes, you can do it yourself or seek a professional's help. Let's explore some guidelines to help you decide what works best for you.

You may consider doing your own taxes if any of the following apply:

1. Your tax situation is relatively simple. This means you have one source of income, like a full-time job, or two sources, such as a full-time job and a side hustle. It could also include having fixed income from sources like Social Security, a small number of investments outside your retirement accounts, and not taking early withdrawals from your retirement accounts. Additionally, doing your taxes yourself could be manageable if you plan to take the standard deduction or make simple itemized deductions.

2. You haven't experienced significant life changes during the year. If you've had minor life changes, like purchasing a home, getting married, or having a child, you might still be able to handle your taxes on your own.

3. You feel comfortable with the process. It's important to note that if there are any errors, you'll be responsible for correcting them during the tax filing process.

On the other hand, you may want to seek the assistance of a professional if any of these things apply:

1. Your tax situation is complex. This could include having a lot of investments outside of retirement accounts, owning rental property, or owing taxes in multiple states.

2. You've undergone major life changes, such as retirement, receiving an inheritance, selling an estate or your home, or going through situations like separation or divorce that impact your tax situation.

3. You own a business. This could involve filing a separate business tax return, reporting income or loss from your business on personal tax returns as a sole business owner, owning a business with employees, or selling your business.

4. You're facing an IRS audit, or if the IRS notifies you of an audit, whether due to owing them money, underreporting income, or other reasons, it's usually wise to seek professional assistance to navigate the process effectively.

5. You want to save time. If you're busy with work, family, or other life situations and want to ensure your taxes are done correctly, seeking the help of a professional can be a valuable time-saving option.

6. You're not comfortable filing taxes on your own. It's essential to remember that the IRS has consequences for not filing your taxes, so if you lack confidence in handling the process independently, seeking professional guidance is a great choice.

Consider these factors and assess your comfort level before making a decision. Remember, the goal is to ensure your taxes are filed accurately and on time, so you can avoid any potential issues with the IRS.

What is the Purpose of Life Insurance?

Life is a beautiful journey filled with moments of joy, love, and laughter. But it's also unpredictable, and as responsible adults, we must prepare for the unexpected. Life insurance is one of the essential tools in your financial toolkit to safeguard your family's well-being. Let's explore the purpose of life insurance and why it's a crucial investment for your family's future.

1. Providing a Safety Net: Imagine life as a tightrope walk. On one side, you have your family's financial security, and on the other, the uncertainties of life. Life insurance acts as a safety net, ensuring that if you were to fall, your loved ones wouldn't be left without a financial cushion.

2. Regular Premium Payments: Life insurance works on the principle of regular premium payments. You pay a certain amount of money to an insurance company at specified intervals, typically monthly or annually. In return, the insurer commits to providing a payment of death benefit to your beneficiaries (those you choose to receive the money) upon your passing.

3. Understanding Types of Life Insurance: There are two main types of life insurance: term insurance and permanent insurance.

4. Term Insurance: Think of this as a temporary coverage option. It's usually more affordable, making it accessible for most people. However, it has a specific term, and if you outlive that term, you will need to renew the policy.

5. Permanent Insurance: This type guarantees lifelong coverage but comes at a higher cost than term insurance.

The beauty of permanent insurance is that it ensures a payout for your family, regardless of how long you live.

6. When to Buy Life Insurance: You might be wondering when is the right time to purchase life insurance. Major life milestones often signal the need:

7. Getting Married: When you say "I do," it's time to think about protecting your spouse's financial future.

8. Buying a Home: A home is a significant investment, and life insurance can help your family keep it if something were to happen to you.

9. Starting a Family: When you welcome a new addition to your family, it's time to ensure their financial security. Remember, life insurance requirements can change with significant life changes. Reviewing your policy periodically is essential to ensure it still meets your family's needs.

10. The Responsible Choice: Life insurance is more than just a financial tool; it's a responsible choice that provides peace of mind for you and your family. It ensures that even in your absence, your loved ones will have the support they need to maintain their quality of life.

Currency Of Conversations

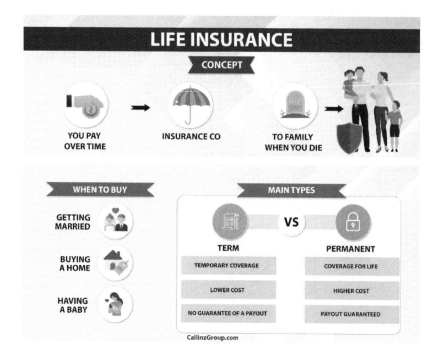

SECTION 3

Debt

Your imagination has the ability to solve your financial problems.

~ Linsey Mills

What Is Debt? What Are the Different Types of Debt?

Now let's talk about debt and its various types. *Debt*, simply put, is when you owe money to someone or a business. Think of it as a financial responsibility or liability you have toward others. When you borrow money, you must pay it back, usually with interest. Interest is the additional amount you owe the lender for borrowing the money.

Now, let's explore the different types of debt and how they work:

1. Secured debt: This type of debt involves borrowing money connected to collateral. *Collateral* is a physical item that reduces the risk for lenders because they can take it if you fail to repay the loan. For example, when you borrow from a bank for a home mortgage, the collateral is usually the house itself. If you fall behind on payments for around six months or more, the lender may initiate foreclosure proceedings and take legal ownership of your home. Similarly, if you default on your car loan, the lender can repossess the car that secured the loan.

2. Unsecured debt: Unlike secured debt, *unsecured debt* does not require collateral. A typical example of unsecured debt is credit card debt. Since there's no specific asset for the lender to claim if you don't pay, unsecured debts generally come with higher interest rates. If you fail to pay your credit card debt, the credit card issuer may sell your delinquent debt to a third-party debt collector. They will then start contacting you for payment, and if you still don't pay, they might take legal action, potentially leading to wage garnishment.

3. Revolving debt: *Revolving debt* refers to an open line of credit where you have a set borrowing limit. If you make the minimum payments on time, you can continue borrowing money with interest. Credit cards are a typical example of revolving debt. However, it's important to note that revolving credit accounts often have higher interest rates than loans. Additionally, some of these accounts may have annual fees, origination fees, and other charges.

4. Nonrevolving debt: *Nonrevolving debt* involves taking out a significant amount of debt, such as a mortgage or student loan, with an agreed-upon interest rate and repayment plan. These types of loans usually have a fixed term and regular monthly payments. Sometimes, there may be prepayment penalties if you want to pay off your loan earlier than the agreed term. Lenders impose these penalties to recoup the interest they would have received if the loan were paid off as per the original schedule. The penalty amount is typically a percentage of the outstanding loan balance during payoff.

5. Zero down debt: This type of debt refers to situations where you can pay in cash but are encouraged to finance instead. An example is the "buy now, pay later" program. However, it's essential to be cautious with these programs as they have some disadvantages:

    - They may encourage impulse spending.
    - Late payment fees may apply if you don't pay on time.
    - Late payments can negatively impact your credit score.
    - Many people spend money they don't have when using these programs.
    - In rare cases, even if you return the item, you may still be required to continue making payments.

Understanding the different types of debt is crucial for managing your finances effectively. It helps you make informed decisions and develop strategies to reduce and eliminate debt over time.

Client Conversation: True Partner

"Many advisors offer advice, but not everyone follows through. I can proudly say that I was one of the fortunate ones who did. Linsey's wisdom and recommendations were like a roadmap, and I followed it diligently. It's one thing to receive advice, but it's another to have a trusted guide who ensures you stay on the right path.

I'm thankful for Linsey's early involvement in my financial journey, and I credit him for the financial stability and peace of mind I enjoy today. He's not just an advisor; he's a true partner in securing your financial future."

What Are Most People Going into Debt For?

Let's talk about the most common debt types that people accumulate. Understanding these types of debt is important to make informed decisions about your finances. Let's dive into each one:

1. Credit card debt: *Credit card debt*, which is quite common in America, occurs when you use a credit card to make purchases but don't pay off the monthly balance. The remaining balance, along with interest, becomes the debt you owe. Credit card companies often offer 0 percent interest for a certain period, like eighteen months, but once that period expires, you must pay interest on the remaining debt. According to RamseySolutions.com, around eight out of ten Americans have a credit card, and the total credit card debt is a whopping $804 billion.

2. Student loans: *Student loans* are loans taken out to pay for higher education, such as college, graduate school, or law school. They have become the fastest-growing debt in America. Approximately 70 percent of students graduate with some amount of student loan debt. These loans are unsecured, which means there are penalties for non-payment, but no collateral is repossessed. They are also nonrevolving, as each loan serves a specific purpose, although multiple loans can be taken out. The average student loan debt is around $40,000, with an average interest rate of approximately 6 percent. It typically takes people about twenty years to pay off their student loans, including the interest.

3. Car loans: *Car loans* are taken out when you need to borrow money to purchase a car. The average car loan debt per household in America is about $32,000. Car loans are revolving and secured debts. This means you borrow a lump sum of money, and the car itself is collateral. If the debt is not paid, the lender can repossess the car and sell it at an auction. They may also sue the borrower for any remaining balance. The average interest rate for car loans ranges from 4 percent to 9 percent for used cars. Typically, people take three to five years to pay off their car loans, including interest.

4. Mortgage: A *mortgage* is a loan that helps people purchase homes. Approximately 52 percent of households in America have mortgages, with a median monthly payment of $1,600. The average mortgage debt is around $202,000. Mortgages are secured loans because the home itself serves as collateral. The lender can foreclose on the property if the debt is not paid. Mortgages are also nonrevolving, as they provide a lump sum to purchase a home. The average interest rate for a thirty-year fixed mortgage is approximately 7 percent, which can vary based on the current economy.

5. Home Equity Line of Credit (HELOC): A HELOC allows you to borrow money based on the equity in your home. *Equity* is the difference between the home's value and the amount owed on the mortgage. By taking out a HELOC, you are essentially trading your home's equity for additional debt. The average American with a HELOC owes about $74,000. HELOCs are considered secured debts because

your home can be repossessed if the debt is not paid. These loans often come with variable interest rates that can increase over time at the lender's discretion.

6. Personal loans: *Personal loans* are borrowed from banks, credit unions, or online lenders for various purposes. People may use personal loans to pay off other debts or cover personal expenses. Around 20 percent of Americans have personal loans, with an average debt of $17,000. Depending on the loan terms, personal loans can be secured or unsecured. They are nonrevolving, meaning they are usually one-time loans. The interest rates on personal loans depend on factors such as credit score, income, and existing debt. Riskier borrowers generally have higher interest rates.

7. Medical debt: *Medical debt* arises when individuals need to pay for healthcare costs and related expenses. It's estimated that around one hundred million Americans have medical debt, with approximately 25 percent of adults owing more than $5,000. Medical debt is considered unsecured and nonrevolving. No collateral is involved, and it often occurs as a one-time expense. However, people can accumulate more medical debt if they have ongoing medical needs or additional procedures. If a medical bill goes unpaid, the healthcare provider may try to collect the money directly or through a third-party bill collector. Unpaid medical bills can negatively impact credit scores if reported to credit bureaus.

Understanding the different types of debt can empower you to make better financial decisions. It's crucial to manage your debt wisely and strive to pay it off promptly to maintain your financial well-being.

Client Conversation Mortgage Payoff:

"When COVID hit, and many were taking advantage of payment holds, I reached out to Linsey Mills, my financial consultant, as I considered it a significant financial decision. I was initially excited about the prospect of not making payments for several months like everyone else in the US.

With enthusiasm, I called Linsey, thinking I was going to follow the crowd and defer my payments for three or four months. However, Linsey had a different perspective. He suggested that instead of postponing payments, we should use this time to pay down my condo's mortgage. I was taken aback, but Linsey was confident in his advice.

To my surprise, Linsey also pointed out that I had some extra funds in my bank account that could be put to good use. He convinced me that it was the right time to pay off my condo completely. I was shocked because I had never owned a property that was debt-free, and I hadn't considered going in that direction before. Thanks to Linsey's guidance, I not only paid off my condo but also shifted my financial trajectory in a more secure and positive direction. I'm truly grateful for his expertise and thoughtful advice."

What about Borrowers Facing Financial Hardships?

When borrowers face financial hardships, they must know that various options are available to help them navigate these challenges. Let's explore a few options: loan modification, forbearance, and deferment.

Loan Modification

A *loan modification* is an agreement between you and your lender that adjusts the terms of your loan. This option is commonly used for home mortgages and aims to make monthly payments more affordable. The great thing is that it's a win-win situation for both parties involved, as it allows you to manage your payments better while helping the lender avoid costly and time-consuming foreclosure procedures.

With a loan modification, your lender may agree to extend the repayment period, reduce the interest rate, switch your loan from an adjustable rate to a fixed rate, or even decrease the principal balance. However, reducing the principal balance is rare since it gives you free home equity. To qualify for a loan modification, you must meet specific requirements, such as missing at least one payment, providing proof of financial hardship, and demonstrating that you can make payments with the modified loan terms.

Forbearance

You can request *forbearance* if you're having trouble repaying your loans due to financial hardships like an illness or job loss. This option primarily applies to mortgages and federal student loans. It's essential to note that during the forbearance period, your loan will continue to accrue interest, which will be added to the overall balance.

In the case of mortgages, your lender may allow you to temporarily reduce or pause your monthly payments while also agreeing not to pursue foreclosure during that time. The terms of forbearance can vary. In some cases, you may be required to repay the entire amount that would have been due during the forbearance period. In other instances, the forbearance may extend your loan repayment period to compensate for missed payments.

For federal student loans, forbearance may be granted if your current income doesn't enable you to make your full monthly payment. Typically, this forbearance lasts for twelve months and allows you to pause making debt payments temporarily. However, it's important to keep in mind that forbearance is a temporary break from paying your loans, and you'll eventually need to resume making payments to repay your loan fully.

Deferment

Deferment is another option available specifically for student loans. Unlike forbearance, which offers a temporary break from loan payments, deferment allows you to postpone payments for an extended period. However, there are specific qualifying events that make you eligible for deferment. These events can include being in school, experiencing economic hardship according to federal regulations, serving in the Peace Corps, being on active duty in the military (or having been active duty within the last thirteen months), being unemployed or unable to find a job, being enrolled at least half time in postsecondary school (beyond high school), being enrolled in graduate school, or being disabled and participating in rehabilitation training. If you have a subsidized loan, interest will not accrue during the deferment period, which can provide some relief.

Remember, it's always best to contact your lenders for more information on the application process and requirements for loan modifications, forbearance, and deferment. They can provide the most accurate and up-to-date information based on your loan.

Financial hardships can be overwhelming, but you can find a path toward financial stability by exploring these options and seeking guidance. As a financial coach, I'm here to support you throughout this journey, so please don't hesitate to reach out if you need further assistance.

What Is Refinancing?

Refinancing is taking out a new loan to pay off an existing one. People often consider refinancing to achieve a lower interest rate or reduce their monthly repayment amount. Switching to a longer-term loan with lower monthly payments can also be an option. However, while refinancing may offer immediate benefits, the total amount you repay over time will likely increase because you'll pay interest for a more extended period.

Let's explore why individuals choose to refinance their loans:

1. Lower interest rate: If your credit score has improved since obtaining the original loan, lenders may be willing to offer you a lower interest rate when refinancing.

2. More affordable payments: Refinancing allows you to adjust the terms of your loan, which can result in more manageable monthly payments. This can be achieved by extending the repayment term or finding a loan with a lower interest rate.

3. Shorter-term loan: Some borrowers opt to refinance to obtain a shorter-term loan. Doing so reduces the time it takes to repay the loan, ultimately saving money on interest payments.

4. Transitioning from variable to fixed rates: Refinancing also offers the opportunity to switch from a loan with a variable interest rate, which fluctuates with the market, to a loan with a fixed interest rate that remains consistent throughout the repayment period.

Now let's explore the different types of loans that people commonly refinance:

- Student loans: Refinancing can be used to consolidate multiple student loans from different lenders into a single loan, often with a lower interest rate, simplifying repayment.

- Personal loans: Some individuals may consider refinancing personal loans to secure better terms, such as obtaining a credit card with a 0 percent APR or taking out another personal loan with more favorable conditions. Remember that some lenders may charge an administration fee, which will be included in the loan balance.

- Credit cards: Refinancing can be an effective strategy to pay off high-interest credit card debt by taking out a personal loan with a lower interest rate. This makes the payments more affordable, as credit card interest can accumulate rapidly.

- Auto loans: If car payments become challenging, refinancing your auto loan can help you secure a lower monthly payment. It's worth noting that eligibility requirements set by banks, such as the car's age, mileage limit, and outstanding balance, may apply.

- Mortgages: Many individuals refinance their mortgages to lower their monthly payments or shorten the loan term from thirty to fifteen years. However, it's essential to consider the potential impact of closing costs associated with refinancing a mortgage.

When it comes to refinancing a home, there are several options to consider:

- Rate and term: Paying off the existing loan and refinancing with a lower interest rate or reduced monthly payments.
- Cash-out: By replacing the current mortgage with a larger one, you can tap into your home equity and receive the difference in cash.
- Cash-in: Making a lump sum payment to the lender when refinancing allows you to qualify for better loan terms.
- No-closing-cost: This option eliminates the closing costs associated with refinancing, but it may result in higher interest rates and monthly payments.
- Reverse mortgage: Available to those with at least 50 percent home equity, a reverse mortgage allows borrowers to borrow against their home's equity, receiving payments from the lender.
- Debt consolidation: Some homeowners refinance and borrow more than their current loan amount to pay off other debts. This can be beneficial for those with substantial debt burdens.

When considering refinancing, keep the following factors in mind:

- Credit score impact: Refinancing involves lenders checking your credit report, which can temporarily lower your credit score. Additionally, remember that refinancing introduces new debt, and lenders will assess your ability to repay this new loan.

- Fees and penalties: Refinancing can come with additional costs, such as closing costs and repayment penalties. Consider these expenses and how they may affect your cash flow.

This information provides a clear understanding of how refinancing works and the various factors to consider. As your financial coach, I'm here to assist you.

What Is Debt Consolidation? How Does It Work?

Debt consolidation is a financial strategy that can help simplify your finances and reduce your debt burden. The idea behind debt consolidation is combining multiple debts into one loan with a lower interest rate. Doing so can save money over time and make your debt more manageable.

Here's how debt consolidation works: Instead of juggling multiple monthly payments and dealing with different interest rates, you take out a new loan to pay off all your existing debts. This new loan, a consolidation loan, typically comes with a lower interest rate than your previous debts. By consolidating your debts, you streamline your payments into one monthly installment, making tracking and managing your finances easier.

One of the advantages of debt consolidation is the potential for more favorable loan terms. In many cases, consolidation loans are secured against collateral such as a home or car. This collateral helps lenders feel more confident lending you money and may result in lower interest rates and more extended repayment periods.

However, it's important to remember that debt consolidation is not a one-size-fits-all solution. It's not the right choice for everyone and requires careful consideration. Before deciding to consolidate your debts, evaluating factors such as the total amount of debt you have, the interest rates on your current debts, and your credit score is essential. These factors will help you determine if debt consolidation is a suitable option for your specific financial situation.

Remember that while debt consolidation can benefit individuals with significant debt and high interest rates, it may not be the best solution if you have a small amount of debt or already enjoy low interest rates on your current debts.

Lastly, it's important to note that debt consolidation is not a magic fix for all financial problems. It should not be seen as a substitute for responsible spending habits and effective budgeting. It's essential to address the underlying causes of debt and develop a solid financial plan to avoid falling into debt again.

As your financial coach, I'm here to help guide you through decision-making and provide personalized advice. If you have any further questions or need assistance with debt consolidation or other financial matters, don't hesitate to reach out.

What Types of Debt Can Be Forgiven?

Debt forgiveness occurs when a lender erases some or all of your debt, relieving you from financial difficulties and struggling to make monthly payments. However, it's important to note that debt forgiveness doesn't necessarily mean all your debt magically disappears. Instead, it often involves agreeing with your lender to pay a reduced debt than what was originally owed.

Debt forgiveness isn't easily obtained. Lenders typically have eligibility requirements for their forgiveness programs. Factors such as your financial situation and the amount of debt you owe significantly determine whether you qualify for debt forgiveness.

When it comes to the types of debts that can be forgiven, unsecured debts such as credit cards, personal loans, or student loans are generally eligible for debt forgiveness. On the other hand, secured debts like mortgages or car loans are not typically eligible for forgiveness. Lenders who hold secured debts usually pursue foreclosure or repossession to recover their funds.

If you're struggling with debt, exploring options you can control before considering debt forgiveness is important. These options include saving more money, living below your means, or even taking on a second job to increase your income. It's about taking the necessary steps to repay the money you borrowed.

Now that you understand the basics, let's discuss some ways debt forgiveness can happen and why. One common form of debt forgiveness is through *bankruptcy*. We'll delve deeper into bankruptcy in the next chapter, but in short, it's a legal process that allows individuals or businesses to release some or all of their debts.

Loan forgiveness programs are another avenue for debt forgiveness. The government, nonprofit organizations, or private entities typically offer these programs. Their purpose is to assist individuals who are struggling to repay their loans. For instance, the Public Service Loan Forgiveness (PSLF) program is a federal program that forgives the remaining balance on federal student loans after making 120 qualifying payments while working full-time for a qualifying employer. It's worth noting that being approved for this program can be highly challenging, with only around 8 percent of applicants successfully qualifying.

In some instances, creditors may choose to forgive debt as an act of generosity or to avoid legal action. For example, a credit card company might forgive a portion of a customer's outstanding balance if the customer is experiencing financial hardship and cannot make their payments. Additionally, if a borrower cannot repay their debt, a creditor may decide to forgive the debt to avoid the costs and hassles associated with pursuing legal action.

It's essential to be aware that debt forgiveness can have tax implications. When debt is forgiven, the forgiven amount may be considered taxable income by the IRS. For instance, if you have $10,000 in credit card debt forgiven, that $10,000 may be deemed taxable income, and you may be required to pay taxes.

Now let's discuss some specific types of debt that are more likely to be forgiven than others.

Student loans continue to be a significant concern for many Americans. There are various programs available for student loan debt relief, each with different eligibility requirements and approval standards. Certain professions, such as nursing and teaching, may offer more options for student loan forgiveness. However, it's important to note that forgiven federal student loan debt may be considered taxable income, and private student loans generally do not qualify for forgiveness.

Medical debt can also be challenging, as it often involves dealing with health issues and financial burdens. Nevertheless, there are programs for medical bill debt forgiveness. Nonprofit hospitals are legally required to have assistance policies. Additionally, the major credit bureaus have announced that paid medical collections will be removed from credit reports, and unpaid medical collections will only appear if they've been in collections for at least a year.

Regarding tax debt, the IRS offers several options to help individuals manage their tax obligations. One such option is the Offer in Compromise (OIC) program, where you can settle your debt for less than the total amount if you can demonstrate that paying the entire sum would harm your finances. Similar to other debt forgiveness programs, qualifying for an OIC can be challenging. It's essential to conduct thorough research and beware of tax debt relief scams.

Regarding mortgage debt, debt forgiveness is relatively rare. However, there are mortgage modification programs where lenders can adjust your original loan to make it more manageable. We discussed this in more detail in a previous section of the book.

Credit card debt forgiveness is also unlikely for most borrowers. However, there are instances when debt settlement can be negotiated, allowing you to pay less than the current owed amount. It's generally best to work directly with lenders for debt settlement rather than relying on debt settlement firms, which may charge high fees and harm your credit score.

In general, debt forgiveness is more likely to be offered to borrowers experiencing financial hardship or those who cannot repay their debts. Borrowers who can consistently make their payments in full and on time are less likely to be granted debt forgiveness.

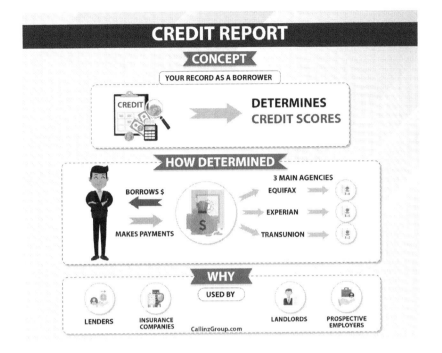

What Is Bankruptcy?

Bankruptcy is a legal process that allows individuals or businesses who cannot pay their debts to seek relief and potentially eliminate or modify those debts. A bankruptcy court oversees it and aims to give debtors a fresh start while protecting creditors' rights.

Individuals or businesses can consider two common types of bankruptcy: Chapter 7 and Chapter 13. Chapter 7, often called *liquidation bankruptcy*, involves selling non-exempt assets to eliminate most, if not all, of the debts. On the other hand, Chapter 13 allows individuals to restructure their debts and create a manageable repayment plan over three to five years.

Bankruptcy can offer significant benefits. It can provide relief from overwhelming debt, putting an end to creditor harassment and collection actions that can cause tremendous stress. It offers a chance for individuals or businesses to start fresh financially, unburdened by their previous debts.

However, it's essential to be aware of the downsides as well. Bankruptcy can be expensive due to court fees and hiring a bankruptcy attorney. It can also have long-term consequences on your financial life, such as lower credit scores and challenges in obtaining credit in the future. The emotional toll of bankruptcy should not be overlooked, as it can impact your mental health, personal relationships, and reputation. It's also worth noting that certain types of debts, like tax debt and student loans, cannot be easily eliminated through bankruptcy. And depending on your career, filing for bankruptcy could have implications in fields like finance or law.

Given these factors, it's crucial to carefully evaluate the advantages and disadvantages of bankruptcy before deciding. Seeking guidance from a qualified bankruptcy attorney is highly recommended. They can provide personalized advice based on your financial situation and help you navigate the complex legal process.

What Is the Most Effective Way to Pay Off Debt?

Two commonly used methods for paying off debt are the debt snowball and debt avalanche. Although both methods aim to reduce and eliminate debt, they differ in their strategies. Let's explore the key differences between these two methods and their pros and cons.

Debt Snowball

The *debt snowball* technique, popularized by financial expert Dave Ramsey, involves paying off debts from smallest to largest, regardless of interest rates. The idea is to first focus on the smallest debt to gain momentum and motivation to keep paying off debts.

With the debt snowball technique, individuals make minimum payments on all their debts except the smallest one. They then allocate any additional money they have toward paying off the smallest debt as quickly as possible. Once the smallest debt is paid off, they move on to the next smallest debt and continue until all debts are repaid.

The debt snowball method is effective because it provides a sense of accomplishment and builds momentum toward paying off larger debts. It's also simple and easy to understand.

The advantages of the debt snowball are as follows:

- Provides a sense of accomplishment
- Builds momentum toward paying off larger debts
- Simple and easy to understand
- The disadvantages of the debt snowball are as follows:
- May pay more interest over time

- Debt payment process may be extended due to higher interest rates

Debt Avalanche

The *debt avalanche* method is a debt reduction strategy that focuses on paying off debts with the highest interest rates first while making minimum payments on other debts. The idea is to pay off high-interest debts first to save more money on interest in the long run. Once the highest-interest debt is paid off, the amount paid toward that debt is then applied to the debt with the next highest interest rate.

The advantages of the debt avalanche are as follows:

- Can save more money in the long run by paying off high-interest debts first
- May pay off debts more quickly because more money goes toward the principal balance rather than interest.

The disadvantages of the debt avalanche are as follows:

- May pay off debts slower if the loan with the highest interest rate is also the largest
- May lose motivation if paying off the loan with the highest interest rate takes a long time

Which method is better?

The most effective method for paying off debt depends on an individual's financial situation and personality. The debt snowball method may be better for those who need quick wins and motivation to stay on track, while the debt avalanche method may be better for those motivated by saving money in the long run. Ultimately, choosing a method that fits one's financial goals and capabilities is essential.

SECTION 4

Saving

Every dollar saved is a step closer to your financial goals and a step further from financial stress.

~Linsey Mills

What Are Some Tips for Saving Money?

Saving money can be challenging for some folks, while others have a knack for it. We all have different spending habits and financial goals, but finding a balance is key whether you're a spender or a saver. After all, we must take care of our needs while enjoying some of life's pleasures. It's all about finding that sweet spot!

Saving money is super important because it helps us build an emergency fund. This fund acts as a safety net when unexpected expenses, like medical bills or home repairs, come knocking at our door. That cushion can ease financial pressure and give you peace of mind. So let's dive into some practical tips that can help you save those hard-earned dollars:

1. Tackle your debt ASAP: Paying off debt should be a top priority. The sooner you settle those balances, the more money you'll save in interest payments.

2. Plan your meals and shop smart: Eating out can be costly, so plan your meals and grocery shopping strategically. This will save you money and also ensure you have healthier options.

3. Cut unnecessary subscriptions and memberships: Take a close look at your subscriptions and memberships. If you're not getting much value from them, cancel them and redirect that money toward your savings.

4. Choose generic over brand-name: Opt for generic products instead of pricier items when shopping. The quality is often just as good, but the price tag is lighter.

5. Explore alternatives to cable TV: Cable bills can add up quickly. Consider switching to streaming services that you use and enjoy. This will help you save money without sacrificing your entertainment.

6. Automate your savings: Set up automatic transfers from your checking account to your savings account. It's an effortless way to save consistently without remembering to do it manually.

7. Adjust your tax withholdings: Talk to a tax professional to see if you can adjust your tax withholdings to increase your take-home pay. This will provide extra wiggle room in your budget.

8. Be energy-efficient: Save on your energy bills by fixing leaks around your home and using energy-efficient LED light bulbs. Every little bit counts!

9. Review your insurance rates: Take the time to compare insurance rates and see if you can find better options. You can save a significant amount by switching to a different provider.

10. Hunt for discounts: Be bold about asking for discounts. Look for special offers or promotions when shopping for various services or attending events. It never hurts to ask!

11. Trim your cell phone bill: Take a close look at your plan and eliminate any extras you don't need. You might be surprised at how much you can save.

12. Challenge yourself with a "no-spend" week or month: Set a period where you challenge yourself to spend minimally or not at all. This is a great way to reset your spending habits and save extra cash.

13. DIY home projects: Attempt simple home improvement projects yourself instead of hiring professionals. This will save you on labor costs, and you might even discover a hidden talent!

14. Brew coffee at home: If you're a coffee lover, consider making your favorite brew instead of hitting the local coffee shop. This will save you a bundle in the long run.

15. Utilize your local library: Instead of buying books or audiobooks, use your local library. You'll have free access to a vast selection of reading and listening material!

16. Opt for a staycation: Instead of spending a ton of money on a fancy vacation, why not plan a relaxing staycation?

Explore your local area, visit nearby attractions, and enjoy well-deserved downtime without breaking the bank.

17. Sell unused items: Look around your house and identify items you no longer need or use. Sell them online or through a yard sale to generate some extra cash.

18. Practice delayed gratification: Train yourself to resist unnecessary expenses. If you find something you want, give it some time before purchasing. Often, you'll realize you didn't need it as much as you thought.

By incorporating these tips into your life, you'll save money, reduce financial stress, and build healthy spending habits. Remember, it's all about finding balance, enjoying life, and securing your future. You've got this!

Linsey Mills with Andrea Stephenson

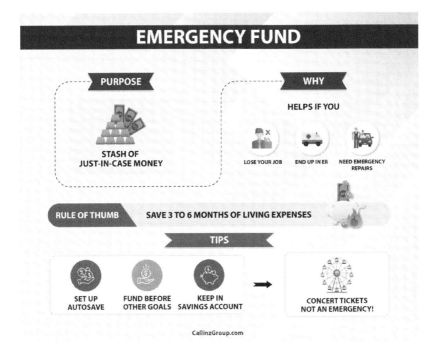

How Do You Save for a Home?

Saving for a home can seem daunting, but trust me, it's possible! Let's break it down into actionable steps to help you get on the path to living in your dream home:

1. Establish a clear savings goal: First, determine the amount you need for a down payment. Aim for 20 percent of the home's price to avoid private mortgage insurance (PMI). This will give you a solid target to work toward. Set a timeframe for achieving your goal, say, within the next two to four years.

2. Reduce your expenses temporarily: Take a close look at your spending habits and find areas where you can cut back temporarily. Consider reducing non-essential expenses like dining out or entertainment. Redirect the money you save toward your down payment fund. Every dollar counts!

3. Increase your income: Consider taking on a side hustle or finding ways to earn extra income. Look for opportunities that align with your interests and skills. For example, explore freelance writing gigs or tutoring opportunities if you enjoy writing or teaching. The additional income can significantly boost your savings for a home.

4. Downsize your lifestyle: Consider downsizing your current living situation to save on expenses. This could mean moving to a smaller apartment or temporarily staying with family or friends to reduce housing costs. You could also explore selling a vehicle if it's optional or moving to a more

affordable area. This adjustment might be temporary, but it can make a big difference in accelerating your savings.

5. Ask for a raise: Prepare for a conversation about a potential salary increase with your employer. Gather specific performance data and highlight the results you've achieved in your projects. Show how you bring value to the company and why you deserve a raise. Sometimes, all it takes is asking and demonstrating your worth to secure that boost in income.

6. Search for a new job: If your current job doesn't provide the financial opportunities you're looking for, consider exploring higher-paying positions in your field. Take the time to develop the skills and qualifications needed for those roles. Networking with professionals in your desired field can also open doors and help you land a better-paying job.

7. Don't quit!: Saving for a down payment requires patience and discipline. There may be times when it feels challenging or slow, but stay committed to your plan. Keep your end goal of homeownership in mind, and remind yourself of the incredible reward that awaits you. With hard work and perseverance, you'll make it happen.

Remember, saving for a home is a journey requiring focus and dedication. But trust me, when you finally step into that dream home, all the sacrifices and efforts will be worth it. Stay positive, stay determined, and you'll achieve your goal of homeownership.

I Need a Car. How Can I Save for It?

I get it, buying a car is a big decision and a significant investment. But don't worry; with a solid plan, you can save up for it and be financially stable. Here are some steps to help you save for your dream car:

1. Determine your down payment: Start by deciding on a target amount you want to spend on your car. Do some research and compare different car models within your budget. Remember, a higher down payment can help you qualify for a loan with better terms and lower interest rates. It can also make your monthly payments more manageable.

2. Choose a car you can afford: Take the time to research different car makes and models. Consider factors like safety features, engine size, gas mileage, and history. A used car is just as good as a new one but comes at a lower price. This can save you some serious money.

3. Budget for car-related expenses: When creating your budget, remember to factor in ongoing expenses like repairs, insurance, and gas. By planning, you'll be prepared for these costs and be aware of the situation. Look for ways to reduce your current expenses and limit unnecessary spending to free up more money for your car fund.

4. Set up a car savings account: Open a separate account dedicated to your car savings. This will help you avoid dipping into those funds for other expenses. Consider choosing a high-interest savings account or a certificate of deposit to let your money grow over time. And to make

saving easier, set up automatic transfers from your checking account to your car savings account.

5. Sell or trade your current car: If you're replacing an old car, consider selling it or trading it in. The amount you get from selling or trading in your current car can be put toward your next one. It's a great way to boost your savings.

6. Choose the right avenue to buy the car: Explore different options for buying a car, such as private sellers, online car retailers, or independent used car dealerships. Whichever route you choose, thoroughly research and inspect the car before making a purchase. It's essential to ensure you're getting a reliable vehicle.

7. Pick up a side hustle: If you're determined to pay for your car in cash, consider finding ways to earn extra money. Look for side gigs or freelance opportunities that align with your skills and interests. The additional income can accelerate your savings and help you reach your car-buying goal faster.

8. Get an inspection: No matter where you decide to buy your car, it's crucial to have it inspected by a trusted mechanic. Avoid sellers who don't allow you to take the car for an inspection. This step will give you peace of mind and help you avoid any hidden issues with the vehicle.

9. Negotiate a reasonable price: When purchasing your car, be mindful of your budget and use your knowledge to negotiate a good deal. Remember, paying for the car in cash gives you more buying power. Compare prices of similar cars, research the car's history, and be willing to

walk away if the price is too high. You have the control to find a great deal.

By following these steps and staying focused on your goal, you'll be well on your way to saving for your dream car. Remember, it's all about planning, budgeting, and making smart financial choices. Happy saving, and soon you'll be cruising in the car you've been dreaming of!

How Do People Successfully Save for Retirement?

Saving for retirement is a smart move that can set you up for a relaxing and joyful future. It's all about having a strategic plan and making intentional choices. Let's dive into some strategies that successful retirees use to save for retirement:

1. Focus on income: Your income is a powerful tool for building wealth. Successful retirees prioritize managing their debts effectively and aim to pay them off before retirement. Minimizing debt gives you more freedom to save for retirement and enjoy your hard-earned money.

2. Set a budget: Creating a monthly budget and sticking to it is crucial. It helps you prioritize your spending and avoid overspending. Successful retirees know their spending habits and stick to their budgets. This way, they can avoid unnecessary expenses affecting their retirement savings.

3. Invest a percentage of income: Investing a certain percentage of your income in retirement accounts is vital. Aim to invest between 12 percent and 20 percent of your income in tax-advantaged retirement accounts, such as a 401(k) or an Individual Retirement Account (IRA). You can make significant progress toward your retirement goals by consistently contributing to these accounts.

4. Think long term: Remember that investing is a long-term game. Successful retirees don't get caught up in day-to-day market fluctuations. Instead, they base their investment decisions on long-term historical performance. Consistency is key when investing, so make regular contributions to

your retirement accounts and stay focused on the bigger picture.

5. Live within your means: Living below your means is a powerful strategy for saving for retirement. Retirement-savvy individuals don't feel the need to keep up with extravagant lifestyles. They prioritize their financial goals, purchase modest homes, pay cash for vehicles and vacations, and avoid unnecessary expenses. This mindset allows them to save more, invest wisely, and reach their retirement goals faster.

By following these strategies, you'll be well on your way to saving for a comfortable and enjoyable retirement. Remember, it's all about making deliberate choices with your income, setting a budget, investing consistently, and living within your means. Start early and stay focused, and you'll be rewarded with financial independence in your golden years.

How Can I Save for Higher Education?

When it comes to saving for higher education, there are several strategies you can consider. Let's dive into some of the top tips for saving for college or graduate studies:

1. 529 plan: One popular option is a 529 plan, an education savings account offering federal and state tax benefits for qualified education expenses. Withdrawals from a 529 plan for college or other qualified higher education expenses are tax-free. Remember that earnings may be subject to income tax and a penalty if the withdrawals are not used for qualified expenses.

2. Mutual funds: Another option is investing in mutual funds, which allow you to put money into a diverse range of securities like stocks and bonds. While mutual fund earnings are subject to annual income taxes, any capital gains are taxed when you sell your shares.

3. Custodial accounts: Custodial accounts are brokerage accounts opened by an adult on behalf of a child. The funds in these accounts can be invested in various securities like stocks, bonds, and mutual funds. This option is excellent for parents who want to transfer assets to their children but maintain control until they reach a specific age. Remember that earnings in custodial accounts are taxed to the minor and may be subject to the "kiddie tax."

4. Coverdell Education Savings Account (ESA): A Coverdell ESA is a tax-advantaged savings account that can be used for qualified education expenses from elementary school through college. Contributions to the Coverdell ESA are

limited to $2,000 per year per beneficiary, and earnings grow tax-free if used for educational expenses. However, it's important to note that the contribution limit is relatively low compared to other savings plans.

5. Roth IRA: While primarily a retirement savings account, a Roth IRA can also be used for qualified education expenses. Contributions to a Roth IRA can be withdrawn tax-free before retirement age if they are used for educational expenses. Keep in mind that contribution limits and earnings withdrawals before age 59 ½ may be subject to income tax and a penalty.

6. Savings account: A traditional savings account offered by banks and credit unions is a basic option for saving for college. While it doesn't offer the same tax advantages as other options, funds in a savings account are easily accessible, and there are no restrictions on how they can be used.

When choosing the best account type for saving for higher education, consider factors like tax benefits, contribution limits, investment options, and how the account may affect financial aid eligibility. Exploring other options like scholarships, grants, and work-study programs is essential, as they can help reduce the amount you need to save.

By exploring these strategies and understanding their implications, you'll be better equipped to make informed decisions and save effectively for higher education.

How Can I Save for a Vacation:

Planning and saving for a vacation can be an exciting journey. Let's explore some steps to help you save money and pay cash for your dream getaway:

1. Travel at the best time: Look at your financial situation before diving into trip planning. If you have any outstanding debts, it's a good idea to prioritize paying them off first. Once that's taken care of, consider traveling during the off season or on less expensive days of the week to save money.

2. Be selective about the destination: Choose a vacation destination that aligns with your preferences and budget. You can seek advice from a travel agent, who often provides their services for free, or look for destinations that offer off-season rates.

3. Consider trip expenses: Calculate the total cost of your trip, including lodging, food, transportation, and flight expenses. Research deals and discounts that can help reduce the overall cost.

4. Budget for the trip: Create a vacation budget by setting up a fund in your budgeting app and establishing a savings goal for your trip. Determine how much you need to save each month and keep track of your progress.

5. Save for the trip: Increase your vacation savings by allocating a specific monthly amount. To determine this amount, divide the total cost of your trip by the number of months until your vacation. Look for ways to boost your income, reduce spending in other categories, or even

consider selling items you no longer need to save more money.

6. Avoid using debt: It's essential to resist using high-interest-rate credit cards to finance your vacation. Doing so can lead to debt and high interest charges. Stick to your budget and pay for your vacation in cash.

By following these steps, you'll be well on your way to saving and enjoying a memorable vacation without worrying about debt or financial stress. Remember, planning and saving ahead of time will make your trip even more enjoyable and relaxing. Bon voyage!

SECTION 5

Investing

Choosing to invest in income-generating assets allows you to break free from the shackles of a limited income, opening doors to a world of possibilities.

~Linsey Mills

What Is Investing and Why Is It Necessary?

Investing is an essential strategy for growing wealth and making money work for you in the long run. While it's true that keeping cash or stashing it away in a savings account is considered safe, investing offers the potential for compounding and long-term growth.

Now, various investment options are available, such as stocks, bonds, mutual funds, exchange-traded funds (ETFs), real estate, and more. Your income, age, and risk tolerance will influence the investment choices that are right for you. For example, if you're starting your career and are younger, your investment objectives might differ from someone approaching retirement.

It's always possible to start investing regardless of your age or income. Even small investments can have a significant impact over time. If you're willing to invest long-term, you can build wealth and enjoy a comfortable retirement.

Let's take a closer look at some of the benefits of investing:

1. Grow your wealth: Investments like stocks, bonds, and certificates of deposit provide returns that allow your money to grow over time, helping you build wealth.

2. Save for retirement: By investing in a diverse portfolio that includes stocks, mutual funds, real estate, or precious metals, you can accumulate funds for retirement that will serve as a source of income when you stop working.

3. Earn higher returns: Investing in stocks, bonds, and other assets offers the potential for higher returns compared to what you'd earn from a traditional savings account.

4. Reach financial goals: The higher returns on your investments can be used to achieve significant financial goals, such as buying a home, starting a business, or funding your children's college education.

5. Build on pre-tax dollars: Investment vehicles like 401(k) plans allow you to invest pre-tax dollars, which means you can save more money than if you were only investing post-tax dollars.

6. Qualify for employer matching programs: Investing in a 401(k) plan can also make you eligible for employer matching funds, giving you free money to boost your investment. This is when your employer contributes a certain amount to your retirement savings plan based on how much you contribute.

7. Start and expand a business: Investing in new business ventures is crucial for business creation and expansion. It's

a way to support entrepreneurs, contribute to job creation, and help bring innovative products and services to the market.

8. Support others: Investing in people and their goals can be a rewarding way to use your money. You can support projects, causes, or organizations that align with your values and make a positive impact.

9. Reduce taxable income: You can lower your taxable income by investing pre-tax dollars in a retirement fund. Additionally, any losses from investments can be applied against gains, reducing your taxable income.

10. Be part of something new: Investing in innovative ventures allows you to be part of cutting-edge projects and ideas. It can be an exciting and rewarding experience, contributing to advancements and breakthroughs in various industries.

Investing involves risk, so it's crucial to do your research, diversify your portfolio, and seek advice from professionals when needed. But with careful planning and a long-term perspective, investing can be a powerful tool for achieving your financial goals and securing a prosperous future.

What Are the Basics of Investing in Stocks?

Let's talk about the basics of investing in stocks. Think of the stock market as this vast store where people can buy and sell ownership pieces of companies that are available to the public. It's like a marketplace where different participants can get involved, from individuals to big companies. You'll find various places where this buying and selling occurs, like the New York Stock Exchange and Nasdaq. Each place has its own set of rules for companies that want to raise money by selling ownership pieces.

Now, imagine the stock market as a mix of a flea market, auction house, and mall all rolled into one. Both parties must agree on a price when they want to buy or sell a piece of a company. This price can change significantly due to factors like the company's earnings and global events.

When the price of a company's stock goes up or down by a significant amount, we use different terms to describe it. A *correction* happens when a group of companies sees a drop of 10 percent to 20 percent in their stock prices. If that group drops more than 20 percent, we call it a *bear market.* Conversely, a *bull market* occurs when the group increases by more than 20 percent after a significant decline. And when the prices of many stocks across different companies suddenly plummet, we call it a *crash*. Lastly, *volatility* refers to when stock prices fluctuate a lot and do so quickly.

You may have heard of stock traders who aim to make money by frequently buying and selling stocks. Another strategy is buying and holding a piece of a company for a long time. We call this long-term investing. It's beneficial because you can make money while using compound interest to earn even more and save money on taxes. It's a good idea to hold onto your investment for at least three to five years, if not longer.

Remember, investing in stocks does come with risks, and it's crucial to educate yourself and stay informed. But by taking a long-term approach and being patient, you can see your investments grow and work toward achieving your financial goals.

How Do I Invest in Stocks as a Beginner?

Investing in stocks as a beginner might feel overwhelming, but don't worry—I've got you covered with six simple steps to help you get started:

1. Choose your investment approach: Determine whether you want to select stocks and funds independently, seek expert guidance, or invest through your employer's 401(k) plan. If you prefer to make independent choices, keep reading.

2. Open an investing account: You'll need an investing account to invest in stocks. You can open a brokerage account if you want to handle your account independently. Alternatively, consider a robo-advisor—an online financial advisor that uses algorithms to provide guidance. Both options allow you to start with minimal funds.

3. Decide between stocks and funds: When investing in stocks, you have two primary options—stock mutual funds or exchange-traded funds (ETFs) and individual stocks. Mutual funds let you buy small portions of different companies in one transaction, while ETFs are like mutual funds but track specific indices like the S&P 500. Individual stocks involve purchasing shares of a particular company.

4. Choose your investment strategy: Once you've settled on stocks or funds, it's time to select an investment strategy. Your strategy should align with your goals, risk tolerance, and time horizon. For instance, if you're investing long-term, a strategy centered around buying and holding stocks for an extended period may be suitable.

5. Set a budget: Establishing a budget for your stock investments is crucial. Determine how much money you can comfortably invest without impacting your immediate expenses. Remember, investing always carries some risk, so only invest funds you can afford to lose.

6. Manage your portfolio: Once you begin investing, monitoring and managing your portfolio regularly is essential. One crucial rule is to build a diversified portfolio, meaning you invest in a variety of stocks and funds to reduce risk. Additionally, stay focused on the long term and avoid making impulsive decisions based on short-term market fluctuations.

By following these steps and staying informed about market trends, you'll be well on your way to confidently navigating the stock market. Investing is a journey, and it's essential to continuously educate yourself and adapt your strategies as you gain experience.

How Do Mutual Funds Work?

When it comes to mutual funds, it's important to choose funds that align with your investment goals. Let's break it down into simple terms. Mutual funds are like a team effort, where people pool their money to invest in various things, like stocks, bonds, and other investment options. These funds are managed by a team of professionals deciding which investments to include. If the fund consists of stocks, it's known as a *stock mutual fund*, while a *bond mutual fund* focuses on bonds. With the guidance of investment professionals, mutual funds can be a wise investment choice.

Here's why mutual funds can be a great way to save for retirement and build long-term wealth:

1. Instant diversification: Mutual funds offer diversification by spreading your investments across many companies. This helps reduce risk since you're not putting all your eggs in one basket.

2. Cost-effectiveness: Investing in mutual funds allows you to access a wide range of stocks without incurring hefty transaction fees. This makes it affordable for investors of all sizes.

3. Professional management: Mutual funds are managed by experts who aim to beat the stock market's returns. These professionals carefully select and manage the investments within the fund to maximize growth potential.

Mutual funds come in different types, such as stock and bond funds. Let's take a closer look at some of them:

- Stock funds: These funds invest in stocks from various companies. Growth funds focus on companies with potential future growth, while value funds look for undervalued stocks that have the potential to increase in value. Income funds target stocks that regularly pay dividends. Index funds aim to replicate the performance of a specific market index, while sector funds focus on specific industries.
- Bond funds: *Bond mutual funds* involve a group of investors buying different bonds with their pooled money. These funds provide exposure to the fixed-income market.
- Hybrid funds: These funds invest in a mix of stocks and bonds. Balanced funds maintain a consistent mix of bonds and stocks, while target-date funds gradually shift from riskier investments to more conservative ones as you approach your retirement date.
- Money market funds: *Money market funds* are invested in short-term debt securities and provide regular interest payments. They are considered low-risk investments but may not offer significant long-term returns.

When investing in mutual funds, choosing funds that match your investment goals and risk tolerance is crucial. Working with an investment professional can help you navigate the options available and make informed decisions.

Remember, understanding what you're investing in is key. By learning about the different types of mutual funds and seeking guidance when needed, you can invest confidently and work toward building your wealth for the long term.

Are Bonds a Good Investment, and How Do They Work?

Let's dive into bonds and explore whether they make a good investment and how they work.

Bonds are financial instruments representing loans made by an investor, typically directed toward government agencies or corporate entities. When you buy a bond, you act as a lender, and the issuer pays you regular interest payments as compensation. At the end of the bond's lifespan, the issuer repays the entire debt to you, resulting in a small profit for the buyer. In the meantime, the issuer has access to funds for their needs. Bonds come with specific terms, including loan details, payment schedules, maturity dates, and other factors that must be followed.

Bonds serve as a way for governments, companies, and municipalities to finance their operations, projects, and other investments. They are bought and sold on bond or secondary markets, with various market factors influencing credit risk, interest rate risk, reinvestment risk, and more.

The trustworthiness of the borrower impacts the desirability of bonds as an investment. For example, the US government is widely regarded as a highly trustworthy borrower. If you lend money to the US government by purchasing a treasury bond, you can be confident they will repay it. This knowledge encourages creditors to invest in bonds issued by the US government, as they can expect to profit from them.

Bonds possess several key characteristics, including face value or par value, coupon rate, coupon dates, maturity date, and issue price. The *face value* represents the amount the bond is worth when it matures or when the loan is fully due. The *coupon rate* denotes the interest rate the issuer must pay based on the bond's face value. *Coupon dates* are when the bond issuer is obligated to make interest payments. The *maturity date* is when the bond reaches its full term and the issuer must repay the face value. Lastly, the *issue price* refers to the initial price at which the issuer sells the bond.

There are four major types of bonds: corporate bonds, municipal bonds, government bonds and treasury bills, and agency bonds. Companies issue corporate bonds, municipal bonds are offered by municipalities and states, government bonds and treasury bills are issued by federal government agencies like the US Treasury, and agency bonds are issued by government-sponsored entities.

Bonds are generally considered less risky than investments like stocks because they provide a predictable amount of money upon maturity. However, it's important to note that interest rates can change, which may make it more challenging to find new bonds that offer comparable returns. Unlike stocks, you can't reinvest the interest earned from bonds.

A sound investment strategy often involves a mix of stocks and bonds. Bonds offer a level of safety and the potential for more predictable payouts. On the other hand, stocks carry more risk since you could lose your entire investment if a company goes bankrupt. If you prioritize a safer investment with more predictable returns, bonds may be a larger portion of your portfolio.

Ultimately, when considering whether bonds are a good investment, it's essential to evaluate your personal financial goals, risk tolerance, and the overall diversification of your investment portfolio. Working with a financial professional can help you determine the right balance between stocks and bonds based on your circumstances.

What Does It Take to Invest in Real Estate?

Let's talk about what it takes to invest in real estate. Real estate encompasses land, buildings, and properties like apartments or farmland. As a real estate investor, your goal is to make money through buying, selling, renting, or leasing land or properties. You can employ different strategies to build up your real estate portfolio, but it's essential to be aware of the risks involved.

One significant risk in real estate investing is the potential for financial loss. For example, if you're a fix-and-flip investor who buys a property to renovate and sell, you could lose money if things don't go as planned. Similarly, owning rental property comes with the risk of not finding tenants or experiencing financial challenges. Other types of real estate investing, such as Real Estate Investment Trusts (REITs) or crowdfunding, also carry risks. Additionally, the value of land or property can decrease if the market slows down.

However, real estate investing can be a path to wealth creation, whether pursued as a full-time job or a side venture. There are several advantages to consider. Real estate offers tax benefits and deductions, and it allows you to have control over your investments. It can also serve as a safeguard against excessive price increases.

There are five main types of real estate investing to explore:

1. Homeownership: Owning your home is a crucial first step in investing in real estate. You can significantly increase your net worth as you pay off your mortgage and continue to fulfill tax and insurance obligations.

2. Rental properties: Owning rental properties can provide extra income but comes with challenges. You must handle tenant management, property maintenance, repairs, and insurance. If you have a long-term investment perspective, rental properties can be a good choice.

3. Buy and hold: This strategy involves purchasing and holding onto a property for an extended period. Investors often rent out the property to generate income while they wait for its value to appreciate before selling it for a higher price.

4. Wholesaling: Wholesaling involves connecting a seller who wants to sell their property below market value with a buyer interested in purchasing it. As the investor facilitating the transaction, you charge a service fee for your work.

5. House flipping: House flipping entails buying, renovating, and selling a property for a profit. The key is to purchase the property at a low price. Flipping houses can be enticing because it offers a quicker turnaround than long-term rentals, but there's also a risk of financial loss.

Now, let's explore six essential steps to follow when investing in real estate:

1. Cash is king: Aim to pay for your investment properties with cash whenever possible. Taking on debt introduces additional risks, and having a substantial amount of risk can put your entire investment at stake.

2. Diversification: It's wise to diversify your investment portfolio beyond real estate. Consider investing in

retirement accounts, mutual funds, or other assets to spread your risk.

3. Save for a down payment: Before purchasing a property, save enough for a down payment. This will help you secure favorable financing terms and improve your chances of success.

4. Location matters: Location is a critical factor in real estate investing. Look for areas with strong job markets and growth potential. Investing in properties near your location allows for closer monitoring and management.

5. Seek professional advice: Consult with real estate agents, lawyers, or accountants specializing in investing. Their expertise can provide valuable guidance and help you make informed decisions.

6. Patience is key: Real estate investing is a long-term game. Don't expect immediate profits. Be patient and invest with a long-term perspective in mind.

Real estate investing can be a fantastic avenue for wealth building, but it requires careful planning and patience. By understanding your options and following these steps, you can make smart investments that will pay off in the long run. Working with a financial coach or real estate professional who can provide personalized guidance based on your specific circumstances and goals is always a good idea.

What Are Commodities and How Do They Work?

Now let's talk about commodities and how they work. *Commodities* are raw materials like corn, flour, oil, and metals bought and sold in large quantities. When people trade commodities, they usually do so through futures contracts rather than physically exchanging the goods. These contracts specify that you agree to buy or sell a commodity at a predetermined price on a specific date.

Investing in commodities can be a great way to diversify your investment portfolio and protect against inflation. However, it's important to note that commodities are highly volatile. Their prices can change rapidly and frequently, making commodity trading quite complex. Weather conditions or political events can significantly impact commodity prices, and predicting these changes can be challenging.

When you buy a commodity like corn or flour, you typically don't think about where it was grown or milled. That's because commodities are often used as raw materials to produce other goods. People who trade commodities try to forecast how the prices of these items will change. They engage in futures contracts by either buying contracts (going long) if they expect prices to increase or selling contracts (going short) if they anticipate prices to decrease.

While physical trading of commodities is possible, most individuals utilize *futures contracts*. These contracts specify the quantity and delivery details of a particular commodity. Users who require raw materials for their production processes, such as food processors, often rely on futures contracts to manage the risk of fluctuating prices. For instance, a corn farmer might sell a futures contract for four thousand bushels of corn at $4 each, to be delivered in ninety days. If corn prices decrease, the farmer will benefit from locking in the $4 price. However, if the price rises to $5, they will miss the potential additional profit.

Investors also engage in commodity speculation, buying futures contracts without intending to possess the commodities physically. They do this if they believe the price of a commodity, such as corn, will rise, allowing them to sell the contract at a higher price. Futures contracts are typically traded on commodity exchanges like the Chicago Mercantile Exchange and the New York Mercantile Exchange.

Commodities are often categorized as hard or soft. *Hard commodities* include metals that require mining or drilling, while *soft commodities* consist of crops or livestock grown or raised. The main types of commodities are agricultural products, livestock and meat, energy products, and metals.

Commodity prices are influenced by changes in supply and demand. For example, a bountiful harvest of a particular crop usually leads to a decrease in price, while a drought can cause prices to rise. Similarly, demand for natural gas increases during cold weather for heating purposes, resulting in price spikes. A warm spell during winter, on the other hand, can depress prices. Some commodities, such as gold, are considered more stable and are often used as reserve assets by central banks.

Commodities tend to be more volatile than stocks or bonds. Some investors use commodities to diversify their investments because they have a negative or low correlation with equities. For example, rising oil prices are often associated with a weaker stock market. Additionally, commodities can serve as a hedge against inflation since high inflation often increases commodity prices. In contrast, stocks and bonds perform better in periods of low inflation.

Now let's discuss the pros and cons of investing in commodities:

Pros:

1. Growth potential: Commodities can provide opportunities for significant growth. If there is high demand for a particular commodity like wheat, its price can increase substantially over time.

2. Diversification: Investing in commodities allows you to diversify your portfolio. While stocks and bonds generally move in the same direction, commodities can behave differently. Therefore, allocating some of your investments to commodities can help protect your overall wealth.

3. Inflation protection: Commodities can be advantageous during periods of inflation. As the cost of goods increases due to inflation, the prices of the commodities used to produce those goods also tend to rise. Investing in these commodities can help you capitalize on the inflationary environment.

Cons:

1. Volatility: Commodities can be highly volatile, experiencing significant price fluctuations. This volatility may not be suitable for investors who are uncomfortable with such risks.

2. No income generation: Unlike other investments, commodities do not generate regular income while you hold them. The potential for returns comes primarily from changes in the commodity's price.

It's essential to consider these pros and cons carefully and evaluate whether investing in commodities aligns with your risk tolerance and investment goals. Working with a financial coach or professional can provide valuable guidance tailored to your circumstances.

I Don't Understand Cryptocurrency. What Is It?

Cryptocurrency is a type of digital money that uses cryptography (mathematical techniques and algorithms) for secure transactions and to control the creation of new units. It's different from the regular money we're used to, as no government or company controls it. Instead, it's tracked by many people worldwide using the internet. You may have heard of Bitcoin and Ethereum—they're the most famous cryptocurrencies, but there are over nine thousand different types out there.

The idea behind creating cryptocurrency, particularly Bitcoin, which was the first one, was to have a new kind of money that didn't rely on banks or governments to control it. It was invented by Satoshi Nakamoto in 2008.

To keep track of all the cryptocurrency transactions and make sure everything is accurate, people use something called a *blockchain*. Think of this as a big book that everyone has a copy of. Every time someone spends cryptocurrency, it gets written down in this book, and then everyone's copy of the book gets updated simultaneously. This helps maintain accuracy and prevent cheating or stealing.

To ensure the security of the blockchain, transactions go through a process called *consensus*. Different types of consensus mechanisms exist, like proof of work and proof of stake. In *proof of work*, computers compete to solve complex math problems, and the first one to solve them gets rewarded with some cryptocurrency. This method requires a lot of computing power and electricity, which can be costly. On the other hand, *proof of stake* is a different approach where people must "stake" their cryptocurrency as collateral to participate in validating transactions. The more you stake, the better your chances of being chosen. Proof of stake is faster and more efficient than proof of work.

When it comes to buying cryptocurrency, it can be a bit tricky because there are so many different types, and you need to do your research. However, it can also be exciting because it's something new and different from traditional money.

When it comes to mining cryptocurrency, that's how new cryptocurrency units are released into the world. Mining involves validating transactions in proof-of-work systems like Bitcoin, but it's getting increasingly difficult as the network grows. It requires a lot of processing power and energy. Proof-of-stake systems, on the other hand, require less computing power, and validators are chosen based on the amount of cryptocurrency they stake.

If you're interested in purchasing cryptocurrency, you can do so through crypto exchanges like Coinbase. Some brokerage platforms like Tastytrade and Robinhood also allow you to invest in crypto.

Now, the big question: Is cryptocurrency a safe investment? Well, that's a topic where financial experts have different opinions. Cryptocurrency can be quite volatile, meaning its value can go up and down rapidly, which makes it risky. Some advisors might argue that investing in government-backed money, like the US dollar, is safer. However, suppose you do want to invest in cryptocurrency. In that case, some advisors suggest only investing a small portion of your money and considering how much you can afford to lose if the investment doesn't go well. It's essential to be cautious and do your due diligence when deciding whether or not to invest in cryptocurrency.

What Are Some Investment Strategies?

Regarding investment strategies, it's essential to have a plan that aligns with your retirement goals and risk tolerance and the amount of money you need to achieve those goals. An investment strategy serves as your roadmap, keeping you focused and ensuring you're moving in the right direction as an investor.

To build a strong investment strategy, you should keep some fundamental principles in mind. These principles include maintaining a long-term perspective, taking advantage of tax-advantaged accounts, being consistent in your approach, focusing on growth, and reducing risk through diversification. Embracing these principles will help you make better investment decisions and increase your chances of long-term financial success.

Now, let's explore some common investment strategies you can consider:

1. Passive investing: This strategy involves buying and holding stocks for the long term without frequently changing your portfolio.

2. Active investing: With active investing, you invest in funds where managers actively select investments based on their research and analysis to try and outperform the market.

3. Value investing: Value investors look for stocks that they believe are undervalued and have the potential to increase in value over time.

4. Growth investing: Growth investors seek out young, growing companies with high potential for future growth.

5. Index investing: Index investing involves investing in broad market indices like the S&P 500 to achieve market returns.

6. Dividend investing: This strategy focuses on investing in companies that regularly pay dividends, providing investors with a steady income stream.

7. Contrarian investing: Contrarian investors go against the crowd by buying stocks or other investments that are unpopular or not favored by the majority.

8. Dollar-cost averaging: This strategy involves regularly investing a fixed amount of money, regardless of market conditions. It helps smooth out the impact of market volatility.

Remember that each strategy has its strengths and weaknesses. Choosing the one that best fits your goals, risk tolerance, and investment objectives is essential.

Having a solid investment strategy is crucial for achieving your retirement goals. By following the fundamental investing principles and selecting a strategy that aligns with your objectives, you can make informed investment decisions that have the potential to lead to long-term financial success. Remember that investing is a marathon, so stay focused, stay consistent, and keep moving forward.

Can You Tell Me More about Passive Investing?

Passive investing is a popular investment approach that many people find appealing. It involves buying a diversified mix of investments and holding onto them for an extended period. The investments typically mirror the performance of a broad group of companies, such as the S&P 500 or the Dow Jones Industrial Average. The aim is not to beat the market but rather to achieve similar returns as the overall group of companies.

Passive investors tend to buy and sell less, often opting for index funds. These funds are designed to replicate the performance of a specific index by investing in various stocks, bonds, or other assets that match the composition of the tracked group of companies. When the group of companies changes, the index fund automatically adjusts its holdings accordingly. This approach allows investors to benefit from the collective success of the group of companies over time.

When selecting index funds, investors have various options, such as equity, fixed-income, commodity, currency, or real estate funds. The choice of funds depends on factors like income or growth objectives, risk tolerance, and balancing one's portfolio. For example, fixed-income bond funds can help offset the volatility of growth stocks, while foreign currency funds can provide a hedge against the depreciation of the US dollar.

Passive investing offers several advantages:

1. It tends to generate positive returns because the stock market generally trends upward over the long term.
2. It is cost-effective since minimal buying and selling is involved, leading to lower transaction fees.

3. It helps to diversify risk because index funds invest in a wide range of assets, spreading exposure across multiple companies or sectors.

4. Investors have the flexibility to choose from different types of index funds, allowing for further diversification and customization of their investment portfolio.

Passive investing is a popular investment strategy for many individuals. By purchasing and holding a diversified mix of investments based on the performance of a group of companies, investors aim to achieve similar returns as the overall market. This approach offers numerous benefits, including long-term profitability, cost efficiency, risk diversification, and the ability to choose from various index funds.

What Is Active Investing?

Active investing is an investment strategy that many people find appealing because it involves buying and selling securities frequently to outperform the market. While it may not be suitable for everyone, it offers unique insights into how individual investors can increase their chances of success.

One fundamental principle of active investing is adopting a systematic, data-driven approach to making investment decisions. By analyzing market data, such as trends and patterns, investors can gain a deeper understanding of market dynamics and make more informed trades. Using data to guide investment decisions can help investors make better choices and outperform the market.

Being active in managing one's portfolio is another important aspect of active investing. This means actively monitoring and adjusting investments when necessary rather than simply buying and holding stocks for the long term. While buy-and-hold strategies can be effective in some cases, active investors believe they can gain an edge by actively participating in the market and seizing opportunities.

Options trading is a tool that active investors may use to manage their investments. Options are financial derivatives that give investors the right to buy or sell an underlying asset at a specific price within a certain time frame. This allows active investors to limit their risk while taking advantage of market opportunities. Using options, investors can create strategies tailored to their specific goals and risk tolerance.

Managing risk is another crucial principle of active investing. Diversifying one's portfolio across different securities, industries, and asset classes can reduce exposure to any single company or sector. This diversification helps protect against losses and increases the likelihood of long-term success.

Lastly, staying disciplined in the investment strategy is vital for active investors. This means sticking to a systematic approach, even when emotions or market fluctuations may tempt investors to deviate from their plan. By staying disciplined and following a well-defined investment plan, investors can avoid making impulsive decisions that could lead to losses, especially during market volatility.

Active, data-driven investing can be a powerful tool for individual investors seeking success in the stock market. By adopting a systematic approach, managing risk, using options trading, diversifying portfolios, and staying disciplined, investors can increase their chances of achieving their financial goals. While it may not be suitable for everyone, active investing offers an alternative to traditional buy-and-hold strategies. It may be worth exploring for those seeking a more proactive investment approach. With the right strategy and approach, individual investors can succeed in the stock market and accomplish their financial objectives.

What Is Growth Investing?

Growth investing is an investment approach focusing on investing in companies experiencing rapid growth. It's an exciting strategy because it offers the potential for significant returns, but it also comes with more risk than other investment types.

The goal of growth investing is to identify companies that are growing faster than the overall market. These companies are often in emerging industries and are considered promising due to their potential for future success. However, their stock prices can be higher because they are so promising.

Growth investors also look for companies that reinvest their earnings into their businesses for further growth. This means these companies may not pay dividends to their shareholders, which can be a drawback for some investors who rely on regular income from their investments. Growth investing is most suitable for individuals who are willing to take on higher risks and have the patience to wait for their investments to grow.

One way to invest in growth stocks is by purchasing mutual funds or exchange-traded funds (ETFs) that track the performance of growth stocks and sectors. These funds hold a diversified portfolio of growth companies, allowing you to invest without picking individual stocks. ETFs are particularly cost-effective for growth investing.

Some popular growth ETFs include the iShares Russell 1000 Growth ETF and the Vanguard Information Technology ETF. These ETFs track the performance of high-growth companies in the United States and globally.

If you prefer investing in individual growth stocks, looking for companies with a solid track record that are experiencing rapid growth is essential. Pay attention to unique products or business models and companies that are already successful in their industries. These factors can increase the likelihood of making profitable investments.

To enhance your chances of success with growth investing, consider the following steps:

1. Diversify your investments: Spreading your money across different companies, industries, and sizes can help mitigate risk while maximizing potential returns.

2. Explore international opportunities: Don't limit your investments to your home country. Investing in companies from other countries can provide additional growth opportunities and help diversify your portfolio.

3. Focus on potential winners: Look for companies with exceptional products or business models or those already established as industry leaders. These companies have a higher likelihood of delivering solid returns.

4. Choose the right fund and be patient: If picking individual stocks seems challenging, consider investing in a well-managed mutual fund or ETF focused on growth stocks. However, being patient is crucial to giving your investments time to grow.

5. Conduct thorough research: Take the time to research the companies you're considering and understand the broader economic landscape. This will enable you to make informed decisions and reduce your overall risk.

Remember that growth investing carries inherent risks, so it's essential to approach it cautiously and make well-informed decisions. However, if you do your due diligence and invest wisely, growth investing can potentially lead to substantial financial gains.

What Is Value Investing?

Value investing is a strategy that many investors use to find undervalued stocks in the market. It involves looking for stocks whose price is lower than their actual value. The goal is to invest in these stocks and profit when their price eventually rises to reflect their true worth.

The key to value investing is understanding the concept of *intrinsic value*. This refers to the actual value of a stock, regardless of what other investors might think it's worth. Value investors search for stocks where the difference between intrinsic value and the current stock price is significant. This difference provides a margin of safety that can help minimize losses if the investment doesn't work out as expected.

Value stocks typically have a lower price than their assets or important financial metrics like revenue, earnings, or cash flow. However, to be considered an excellent-value stock, a stock must have additional attractive characteristics. This could include a well-established business with a long history of success, consistent profitability, stable revenue streams (even if they're not growing rapidly), and even dividend payments.

It's essential to exercise caution when searching for value stocks. While some stocks may initially appear attractive, they could become *value traps*. These stocks seem like suitable investments but end up experiencing declines in share price. To avoid falling into value traps, investors should focus on a company's sales and earnings growth prospects in the months and years to come.

Value investing requires thorough research and patience. While the potential returns can be significant, it often takes time for a value stock to be repriced to a more appropriate and higher level. Patience is key to allowing the market to recognize the stock's actual value.

Here are some tips that successful value investors use:

1. Focus on buying businesses, not just stocks. Look at a company's fundamentals rather than getting caught up in market trends.//
2. Invest in companies that you understand well. Avoid complex businesses with high levels of uncertainty.
3. Pay attention to the quality of management. Well-managed companies with strong leadership can add value to the business, while poor management can harm even the most solid financials.
4. Rather than diversifying too much, value investors often concentrate on a few stocks they know well.
5. Thoroughly research the companies you're considering for investment. Understand their financials, competitive advantages, and industry dynamics.

Value investing is suitable for investors who want to minimize the risk of permanent losses while increasing the likelihood of positive returns. There may be a better approach for those who prefer to invest in trendy or high-growth companies, as value stocks typically have slower growth opportunities. However, value investing can be a profitable long-term investment strategy for those willing to put in the work and exercise patience.

What Is Dividend Investing?

Dividend investing is a strategy that involves investing in stocks of companies that regularly pay out dividends to their shareholders. It's a way to generate consistent returns over time.

When a company earns profits, it has several options for what to do with that money. One option is to invest it in research and development or save it for future needs. Another option is to distribute some of those profits to shareholders as dividends. Dividend income is similar to earning interest on a savings account. For example, if you own one share of stock worth $100 with a 5 percent annual dividend yield, the company will pay you $5 annually.

Many investors find dividend income appealing because it provides a steady and reliable way to grow their investments. It can be particularly beneficial for saving for retirement or creating a source of funds later in life.

However, there are some important considerations to consider when it comes to dividend investing. First, dividends are not guaranteed, and companies can change or even eliminate them at any time. It's essential to assess a company's financial health and stability before investing in its dividend-paying stocks. Additionally, companies that pay dividends tend to be larger and more established. Still, they may grow slower than smaller companies re-investing their earnings for future growth.

Dividend investing involves investing in individual stocks or index funds that pay dividends. Dividends are payments made by companies to their shareholders, typically out of their profits. Many large companies, including 77 percent of stocks in the S&P

500, pay dividends. While the current dividend yield of the S&P 500 is around 1.70 percent, which is lower than in the past, it still tends to be higher than the interest rates of savings accounts or Treasury bonds.

Investing in dividend-paying stocks allows you to receive dividends and potentially benefit from the compounding effect. By reinvesting the dividend income into buying more shares of the same company, your investment grows faster, leading to greater overall returns.

There are also tax advantages associated with dividend investing. The IRS treats dividends differently depending on whether they are qualified or unqualified. *Qualified dividends* are taxed at a lower rate for long-term investments, while *unqualified dividends* are taxed at the same rate as regular income. Most dividends paid by companies in the US are considered qualified dividends.

When picking dividend stocks, it's important to consider factors beyond the dividend yield. While a high dividend yield may seem attractive, it's essential to assess the company's underlying health and whether it can sustain its dividend payments. Reliability is critical, so you should review the Dividend Aristocrats, which are stocks with a track record of consistently increasing their dividend payments over time.

If you want to pursue dividend investing, there are three main strategies you can consider:

1. Target high dividend yields, which is a classic approach.
2. Focus on stocks with a long history of increasing dividends, indicating a commitment to shareholder returns.

3. Look for companies with low payout ratios, meaning they return more money to shareholders than they earn.

Dividend investing can be rewarding for those seeking regular income and long-term growth. However, as with any investment approach, it's crucial to conduct thorough research, assess the financials and stability of the companies you're considering, and align your investment decisions with your overall financial goals and risk tolerance.

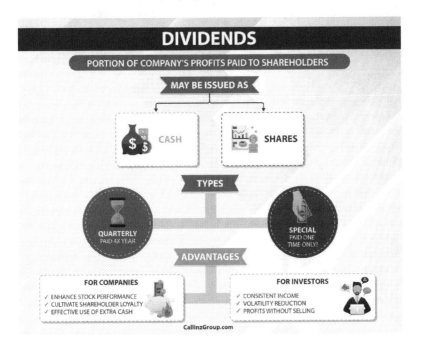

What Is Contrarian Investing?

Contrarian investing is all about going against the crowd and making investment decisions that differ from what most other investors are doing. Instead of following the herd and buying or selling based on popular sentiment, contrarian investors take a different approach. They may choose to buy when others are selling or sell when others are buying.

To succeed as a contrarian investor, you need to put in the effort to conduct thorough research and identify opportunities that other investors may be overlooking. It can be time-consuming and require careful analysis, but it can also be gratifying if you make the right decisions.

One famous example of a contrarian investor is Warren Buffett, who once said, "Be fearful when others are greedy, and greedy when others are fearful." This means that when everyone is jumping on the bandwagon and the market is soaring, it's wise to exercise caution and avoid getting caught up in the frenzy. On the other hand, when fear is rampant and the market is plummeting, that might be an opportune time to consider buying.

Contrarian investors often seek opportunities that are out of favor with the majority. They look for stocks or sectors undervalued or unloved by the general public and then make investments based on their belief that market sentiment will eventually change. It requires patience because it may take time for the market to catch up with their perspective.

For instance, if most investors are optimistic about the economy and anticipate a booming stock market, a contrarian investor may believe that the economy won't grow as fast as expected and that the market is overpriced. In response, they might choose to sell stocks or invest in assets they believe will perform well if the market experiences a downturn.

Contrarian investing is not suitable for everyone, as it carries risks and it demands extensive research and patience. However, it can also be highly rewarding for those willing to take on the challenges. By going against the crowd, contrarian investors have the potential to identify opportunities that others may overlook, and capitalize on them when the market eventually aligns with their viewpoint.

Contrarian investing can be attractive for a couple of reasons. First, when it works, it allows investors to identify market inefficiencies or mispriced assets that need correction. This can lead to significant gains if the investor has the patience to wait for their predictions to come true. For example, buying stocks during a market downturn, known as a *bear market*, can be a contrarian strategy that pays off when the market eventually rebounds.

Second, contrarian investing can be intellectually satisfying. It requires independent thinking, in-depth research, and the ability to challenge popular beliefs. When a contrarian investor's predictions prove correct, it can bring a sense of personal fulfillment beyond just financial gains.

However, contrarian investing also comes with its drawbacks. Developing a contrarian viewpoint takes time and effort. It requires the investor to go against the prevailing sentiment, which can be mentally and emotionally challenging. Additionally, it may require tying up funds in investments that may not yield immediate returns, which can be a disadvantage compared to other investment strategies.

Contrarian investing is not for everyone due to the level of commitment and research it demands. While it can be tempting to prove others wrong, for the contrarian strategy requires patience and precise timing of buying and selling decisions to pay off.

What Is Index Investing?

Index investing is a type of investment strategy where you try to match the performance of a specific market index. You know, those indices like the S&P 500 or the Dow Jones Industrial Average that you often hear about on the news? With index investing, you buy the same stocks or bonds that make up the index or invest in a fund that closely follows the index. The cool thing about this approach is that it's passive, which means you don't have to spend time and energy picking which stocks or bonds to buy and sell. Instead, you rely on the overall market performance to do well over time.

There are some significant advantages to index investing. Research has shown that it often outperforms active management, where people try to handpick winning investments. By not getting caught up in choosing winners and losers, index investors avoid the biases and uncertainties of active management. Index funds usually have lower fees than actively managed funds, and they can be more tax efficient too.

Another benefit of index investing is that it helps you diversify your investments. Instead of putting all their eggs in one basket and buying a few individual stocks or bonds, index investors buy many different ones. For example, if you invest in the S&P 500 index, you're spreading your money across 500 large US companies. Doing so reduces the risk of losing money if one company doesn't perform well.

Now, there are different ways you can invest in an index. One option is to buy all the stocks or bonds in the index, which can be expensive and time-consuming. Another approach is to buy just the most essential stocks or bonds in the index or a sample of them. But if you prefer a hands-off approach, you can invest in a fund that does all the work for you. These funds bundle all the stocks or bonds in the index into one security, making it easier for you to invest.

However, it's important to note that index investing does have some limitations. Some index funds are based on market capitalization, which means that the performance of the largest companies in the index can significantly impact the fund's overall performance. If those big companies don't do well, it can affect the entire index. Also, index investing doesn't take into account specific investment strategies like identifying undervalued stocks or investing in companies with good momentum. These strategies, known as *smart beta*, can sometimes offer better risk-adjusted returns than index investing.

If you're interested in investing in index funds, here are some steps you can follow:

1. Think about your investment goals. If you want to make money quickly and are comfortable taking risks, you might consider investing in individual stocks or cryptocurrency. But index funds could be a great option if you're looking to grow your money steadily over time, especially for things like retirement savings.

2. Do your research. Take a look at the different index funds available to you. Consider factors like the size of the companies, their locations, the industries they operate in, and the types of assets they have.

3. Choose your index funds. Once you've decided which index you want to track, it's time to choose the specific index fund you want to buy. Pay attention to the costs associated with each fund because lower costs mean more money stays in your pocket. You can purchase index funds directly from a mutual fund company or brokerage.

4. Decide where to buy your index funds. Consider factors like the selection of funds, convenience, trading costs, impact investing options, and whether commission-free options are available when choosing where to buy your index funds.

5. Make your purchase. To buy index funds, you'll need to open an investment account through the brokerage you selected in step 4. Once your account is set up, you can buy the index fund right from that account.

Remember, index investing can be a wise and relatively simple way to invest, but it's always a good idea to do your homework and understand the specific index funds you're considering.

What Is Investment Analysis?

Investment analysis is a method to help you determine whether an investment is worth your money. It's like detective work that experts use to assess the profitability and risk of an investment before diving in. There are four main types of investment analysis: bottom-up, top-down, fundamental, and technical.

One way to approach investment analysis is by starting with the big picture and working your way down, known as the *top-down approach*. You look at the overall economy, market trends, and other factors to figure out which investments have the potential to perform well. From there, you can narrow down your choices and select specific investments.

Another approach is the *bottom-up method*, where you focus on individual investments. You zoom in on a company's financial health, management quality, and growth prospects. By evaluating these factors, you can decide whether it's a good investment and how it fits into your overall portfolio.

Now let's talk about fundamental analysis and technical analysis, two popular methods used in investment analysis. Fundamental analysis involves analyzing a company's financial health, its competitive position in the market, and the broader economic outlook. The goal is to find undervalued stocks compared to their true worth. On the other hand, technical analysis focuses more on patterns in stock prices and other data to predict future performance. Day traders often use this method to make buy-and-sell decisions.

When conducting investment analysis, there are several factors to consider: For example, the price you pay for an investment, the length of time you plan to hold it, and how it fits into your overall portfolio. It's crucial to align your investments with your goals, risk tolerance, and financial situation.

For instance, if you're a young adult working for a company, you might consider investing in mutual funds or individual stocks. On the other hand, if you're a retired adult seeking stability, safer securities like fixed deposits and government bonds might be more suitable. Investment analysis helps both individuals and big companies manage their portfolios effectively.

If you're considering investing in a mutual fund, look at its past performance compared to other funds and the overall market. Consider the fees associated with the fund and its types of investments.

It's important to remember that investing is not a one-size-fits-all approach. Everyone has different goals, timelines, and financial situations. So finding investments that align with your unique circumstances is crucial.

Additionally, reviewing your overall investment strategy as part of investment analysis is wise. Take a step back and evaluate why you made certain investments, how they are performing, and whether any adjustments are necessary.

Investment analysis has its advantages. It helps individuals make informed decisions about their money, and experts can thoroughly research securities to assess their sustainability and growth potential. However, investment analysis can be complex and requires financial knowledge. It also comes with unpredictable risks; external factors like government policies can impact its effectiveness. Despite these challenges, investment analysis empowers individuals to make wise investment decisions and maximize their financial potential.

If you need assistance with investment analysis, it's a good idea to seek help from a professional like a financial advisor. They can provide guidance tailored to your specific needs and help you navigate the complexities of investment analysis.

Remember, there are many ways to approach investment analysis, and what works for you may differ from what works for others. The key is to consider your investments carefully, align them with your goals, and make choices that make sense for your unique situation.

How Does Fundamental Analysis Work?

Fundamental analysis is a way to assess whether a company is a good investment by examining its financial statements and other relevant factors. It involves digging into the company's earnings, debts, and management quality. It also considers broader economic factors such as interest rates and employment rates. The ultimate goal is determining if the company's stock is worth investing in. By analyzing all this information, investors can make informed decisions about buying or selling the company's stock.

Let's talk about how to actually perform fundamental analysis. There are two common approaches: top-down and bottom-up.

The *top-down approach* looks at the big picture first. It considers the overall economy, including GDP growth, unemployment, and interest rates. Analysts can predict which industries or sectors are likely to perform well by analyzing these macroeconomic indicators. Based on these predictions, they select specific stocks within those industries to invest in.

On the other hand, the *bottom-up approach* focuses on individual companies. It involves analyzing a company's financial statements to assess its financial health and potential as an investment. This includes evaluating factors like revenue, expenses, assets, and liabilities. By understanding the company's financials and its products or services, analysts can determine whether it's a suitable investment.

Fundamental analysis considers both qualitative and quantitative factors. *Qualitative fundamentals* are intangible aspects like the company's business model, competitive advantages, management quality, and brand strength. These factors play a significant role in a company's long-term success. On the other hand, *quantitative fundamentals* are measurable characteristics like earnings per share (EPS), which indicates the company's profitability. By considering both qualitative and quantitative fundamentals, investors can estimate the intrinsic value of a company's stock.

It's worth noting that fundamental analysis has its variations and nuances, and successful investors like Warren Buffet and Benjamin Graham have their approaches. However, they often emphasize taking a long-term perspective and investing in companies with substantial competitive advantages, strong management teams, and promising growth prospects.

Ultimately, fundamental analysis helps investors make informed decisions based on a deep understanding of a company's financials, industry trends, and economic factors. It's important to remember that fundamental analysis is not a crystal ball that guarantees success, as there are always risks involved in investing. However, conducting a thorough analysis can improve your chances of making sound investment choices aligned with your long-term goals.

If you find fundamental analysis overwhelming or need assistance, consider consulting with a financial coach or advisor who can provide guidance tailored to your specific needs and help you navigate the complexities of investment analysis.

Investing is a journey, and fundamental analysis is a valuable tool to help you make informed decisions and build a solid investment portfolio.

How Does Technical Analysis Work?

Technical analysis is a method used to predict the future value of stocks or other investments by analyzing their past performance. It studies historical price patterns and market data to identify trends and make informed trading decisions. While technical analysis can be applied to any traded investment with available historical data, it's important to note that it cannot predict the outcomes of new stocks.

Many analysts and investment bankers rely on technical analysis, but it's not exclusive to them. Even individual investors who buy or sell stocks can use this technique to gain insights into potential investment opportunities.

To get started with technical analysis, you need to grasp the core principles, such as market action, price trends, and historical patterns of investor behavior. Understanding key aspects of a stock, including market price, opening high/low, and closing high/low, is crucial for identifying trends.

Once you have a solid foundation in technical analysis and a good grasp of stock characteristics, you can look for trend indicators by analyzing specific timeframes and searching for patterns. Analysts often examine various trend indicators, such as chart patterns, cycles, support levels, and resistance levels. These indicators help predict whether an investment's value will likely increase or decrease.

It's worth mentioning that technical analysis differs from *fundamental analysis,* another common approach to predicting stock performance. While technical analysis focuses on historical price movements and patterns, fundamental analysis examines a company's financial health and economic factors to assess its intrinsic value.

In reality, both technical and fundamental analysis have their strengths and limitations. Technical analysis may sometimes overlook significant economic changes, while fundamental analysis may only partially capture investor behavior. Many market participants combine both approaches to understand potential market movements comprehensively.

When engaging in technical analysis, there are several essential steps to consider. First, it's crucial to identify trends, such as *uptrends* (rising prices), *downtrends* (falling prices), or *sideways trends* (fluctuating prices within a range). Additionally, understanding support and resistance levels is crucial, as they indicate whether prices are likely to reverse or continue. Support represents a level where demand for a stock exceeds supply, while resistance represents a level where supply surpasses demand. Breaking out from support or resistance levels can lead to continued movement in either direction.

Volume analysis is another important aspect of technical analysis. Analysts can confirm the strength of ongoing price movements by examining trading volume, which represents the number of shares traded in a specific period. *Candlestick patterns*, which display price action visually, are also valuable tools for identifying potential trend continuations or reversals.

By understanding these technical indicators and incorporating them into your analysis, you can make more informed trading decisions and potentially minimize risk.

Remember, technical analysis is not foolproof and does not guarantee accurate predictions. It's always prudent to conduct thorough research, consider other relevant factors, and seek guidance from professionals or financial advisors who can help you make well-informed investment choices based on your specific goals and risk tolerance.

Technical analysis offers a unique perspective on market trends and can be valuable in your investment toolkit. It can contribute to a more comprehensive understanding of potential investment opportunities when used in conjunction with other analysis methods.

SECTION 6

Retirement

Retirement is when your financial statement says: Relax I'll take it from here.

~ Linsey Mills

How Do I Save for Retirement?

Planning for retirement is an important process that sets you on the right path to a secure future. Let's break it down into simple steps to help you take action and achieve your retirement goals.

First, you must determine how much money you will need to maintain your desired lifestyle during retirement. Consider factors like inflation and estimate how long your retirement might last. Once you have a target amount, subtract any expected income from sources like Social Security or pensions. This will give you a clear idea of how much you need to save. To make this calculation more manageable, you can use online retirement calculators. Once you know your monthly savings target, create a budget to ensure you're consistently setting aside that amount. Regularly monitor your progress and make adjustments as necessary. Starting early and making informed decisions is key to enjoying a comfortable retirement.

Next, aim to invest between 12 percent and 20 percent of your income into long-term investments such as stocks and mutual funds. Additionally, take advantage of retirement savings plans like a 401(k) or Roth IRA. These accounts offer tax advantages and allow your savings to grow without being taxed until you use the money in retirement. It's essential to continue investing for retirement while also saving for other goals, such as your children's education or paying off your home. You can increase your retirement savings once your mortgage is paid and your children have left the nest.

For instance, say you earn $60,000 annually and save 15 percent of your income for twenty-five years. In this scenario, you could accumulate around $1.2 million for retirement. Stretch it to thirty years, and you could have $1.9 million without any additional salary raises.

Remember, it's best to rely on the growth of your retirement savings rather than depleting your savings directly. A financial advisor can assist you in calculating how much you should save each month, considering factors like inflation, fees, and taxes.

Investing for the long term is a smart strategy when saving for retirement. Here are some reasons why it's advantageous:

1. Long-term investing helps you make rational decisions, avoiding emotional impulses that could harm your investments.
2. Historical data shows that long-term investors are more likely to make profitable returns.

3. Long-term investing allows you to benefit from *compounding*, reinvesting your profits over time, generating even more income.
4. Anyone can be a long-term investor, and it's a straightforward approach to wealth accumulation.
5. Investing for the long term reduces stress and promotes better sleep at night.
6. Over time, you can correct mistakes by sticking with solid companies and adding to your investments.
7. Long-term investing often leads to lower taxes compared to frequent trading.
8. Commissions are relatively simple for long-term investors.
9. Investing for the long term lowers your investment risk and minimizes the chance of missing out on significant gains.

As you approach the age of sixty, it's wise to consider obtaining long-term care (LTC) insurance. This insurance helps cover the costs of nursing home care or in-home assistance should you need it in your later years. Including the cost of LTC (long-term care) insurance in your retirement budget safeguards the money you've saved. So make sure to factor it in when planning.

What Are the Different Types of Retirement Plans?

Regarding retirement planning, several options are available, each with benefits and considerations. Understanding these different retirement plans can be overwhelming, but I'm here to help you navigate them.

First up, we have the 401(k). Companies commonly offer this retirement plan as an employee benefit. With a 401(k), you can contribute a portion of your paycheck to the plan, and your employer may match your contributions. One significant advantage is that the money you contribute is deducted from your taxable income, which can provide immediate tax savings. Your 401(k) funds grow tax-free until you withdraw them in retirement. Just keep in mind that there are contribution limits, which were set at $20,500 in 2022, and generally, you can't withdraw the funds penalty-free before the age of 59½.

Next, we have the traditional IRA (Individual Retirement Account). This is a savings plan available to almost anyone with taxable income, regardless of whether they have an employer-sponsored retirement plan or not. Similar to the 401(k), contributions to a traditional IRA can provide tax deductions, reducing your taxable income. The funds in the account also grow tax-free until withdrawal. However, the contribution limit for traditional IRAs is lower than a 401(k), set at $6,000 in 2022.

Now, let's talk about the Roth IRA. With a Roth IRA, you contribute after-tax income into the account, meaning you don't get an immediate tax deduction. However, the significant advantage is that qualified withdrawals in retirement are tax-free. This can be particularly beneficial if you expect your retirement tax rate to be higher. Like the traditional IRA, the contribution limit for a Roth IRA is $6,000 in 2022.

If you're self-employed or a small business owner, consider a SEP IRA (simplified employee pension individual retirement account). This retirement plan allows you to contribute up to 25 per of your income or $61,000 in 2022, whichever is lower. Similar to other retirement plans, contributions to a SEP IRA are tax-deductible, and the funds grow tax-free until withdrawal.

Small businesses with up to one hundred employees also have simple IRA and simple 401(k) options. These retirement plans offer more straightforward and less costly alternatives for employers to provide retirement benefits. Both plans allow tax-deductible employee contributions, and the funds grow tax-free until withdrawal. The contribution limit for a simple 401(k) in 2022 is $13,500, and the same limit applies to a simple IRA.

Lastly, if you're self-employed with no employees other than a spouse, you should explore the solo 401(k) option. This plan allows you to contribute both as an employer and an employee, enabling higher contribution limits. In 2022, the maximum contribution for a solo 401(k) is $58,000, or $64,500 if you're fifty or older. Contributions to a solo 401(k) are tax-deductible, and the funds grow tax-free until withdrawal.

Remember, each retirement plan comes with its own set of rules regarding taxes, contribution limits, and withdrawal restrictions. It's important to consider your specific circumstances and goals when selecting the right retirement plan for you.

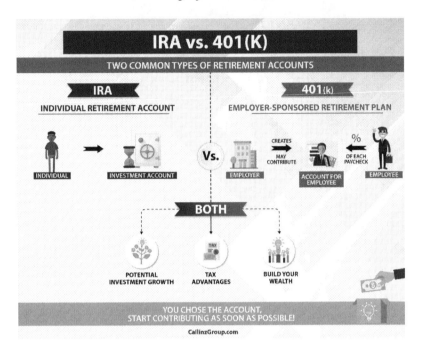

What Are Options for Retirement Income?

When you enter retirement, your regular job income will no longer be there, but it's crucial to have a plan for generating the money you'll need to support your lifestyle. Luckily, there are several options available to you for retirement income. Let's explore the most common methods:

1. Social security: Social security is a valuable income resource for most people. The great thing is that you can't outlive Social Security; it even comes with a cost-of-living adjustment. The longer you wait to start collecting, the more you'll receive. However, it's worth noting that certain types of jobs may reduce your Social Security benefits. We'll delve into Social Security in more detail later, so don't worry.

2. Pensions: If you've worked in a job that offers a pension, you're in luck. A pension is like a regular paycheck you'll receive every month for the rest of your life or your spouse's life. Even if your employer goes out of business, private-sector pensions are insured by the Pension Benefit Guaranty Corporation. Some people even use their savings to create their own pensions by purchasing an immediate annuity.

3. Retirement accounts: Retirement accounts such as 401(k)s and IRAs allow you to save money specifically for retirement. The best part is that you only pay taxes on this money once you withdraw it during retirement. Some employers even contribute extra money to your 401(k), helping you save more. However, remember that when you

retire and start taking money out, you'll have to pay taxes on those withdrawals. Additionally, once you reach seventy-two years of age, you'll be required to take out a certain amount each year to avoid tax penalties.

4. Roth accounts: Roth accounts can be a smart way to save for retirement. With a Roth 401(k) or Roth IRA, you pay taxes on the money you contribute upfront. However, when you withdraw the money later, you won't owe any taxes. This means your money can grow tax-free and you can enjoy tax-free withdrawals in the future. Furthermore, Roth IRAs don't have any rules about when you must start taking money out, so you can let your money continue growing for as long as you desire.

5. Paid-off home: If you own your home and have paid off your mortgage, congratulations! You no longer have to make monthly payments to the bank for your house. While you'll still have to cover taxes and insurance, these expenses will be significantly lower than what you used to pay for your mortgage or rent. If you need money in the future, you can consider borrowing against the value of your home or selling it to downsize, allowing you to put the extra funds into your retirement savings.

6. Stocks and mutual funds: As you approach retirement, it's wise to invest in less risky assets. However, if you're healthy and expect a long retirement, it's still beneficial to keep some of your savings in the stock market. This allows your money to grow and keep up with inflation. Remember to save the money you'll need soon in a safer investment.

Additionally, consider your comfort level with risk when determining how much to invest in stocks.

7. Bonds: Bonds are generally less risky than stocks and can be a good investment for retirees. Bonds typically provide a fixed income stream, and the likelihood of losing your money is low. Certain types of bonds, like Treasury inflation-protected securities (TIPS), offer guaranteed returns higher than inflation. Moreover, investing in certain bonds, such as municipal bonds, can help you save money on taxes.

8. Savings accounts and CDs: Many retirees prefer to keep some of their money in savings accounts or certificates of deposit (CDs) as a safe and reliable place to save. These options are backed by the government, ensuring that your money remains secure even if something happens to the bank. Although the interest rates may not be high, you can have peace of mind knowing that you can easily access your funds when needed.

9. Part-time job: Working part-time during retirement is a popular choice for many individuals. It can provide additional income, help supplement your retirement savings, and offer a sense of purpose and enjoyment. Furthermore, part-time jobs can sometimes include benefits like health insurance or a 401(k) match. Additionally, working after retirement can even help increase your Social Security benefits.

10. Real estate: Investing in real estate can be an excellent option if you need additional income during retirement.

Rental properties can generate a steady income stream, and managing them yourself can increase your earnings. By carefully selecting properties at favorable prices and terms, you may earn more money than traditional investments.

11. Small business: Instead of retiring completely, many people are choosing to start their businesses after turning 65, calling it "encore entrepreneurship." This allows them to continue utilizing their skills and experience while creating a fulfilling small business.

Here are some ideas to consider for starting your own business after retirement:

- Open a bed-and-breakfast and offer guests a warm, welcoming experience with excellent accommodations and delicious breakfasts.
- Become a consultant and provide specialized skills and knowledge to various industries.
- Purchase a franchise with built-in branding, marketing materials, and business plans.
- Start a tutoring business that allows you to set your hours and rates.
- Utilize your hobby in photography to start a small business.
- Become a private tour guide and share your knowledge and love for a particular place with others.

Remember, when planning for retirement, balancing risk and security is crucial. Some methods of generating retirement income are more dependable, while others offer growth potential. The best approach often combines these methods to ensure you have enough money to enjoy your retirement years comfortably.

How Do I Make Sure My Retirement Income Lasts?

Let's explore some strategies to help you achieve that goal of consistent and sustainable retirement income.

First things first, it's essential to pay off all your debts before you retire. Carrying debt into retirement can throw off your budget and put unnecessary strain on your finances. Take a moment to list all your debts and work on paying them off as soon as possible. If you can't pay off everything before retiring, consider working longer or downsizing your home to free up some funds.

It can be helpful to ease into retirement gradually when transitioning into retirement. Consider reducing your work hours or taking on a side business you enjoy. This way, you can continue to generate some income while adjusting to your new lifestyle. It's also wise to be conservative with your withdrawals from your retirement savings. Working with a financial advisor can help you create a plan that suits your unique situation.

Speaking of financial advisors, it's essential to understand your financial situation clearly. Work closely with a financial advisor to determine how much you've saved for retirement and your future needs. Many people make the mistake of guessing their retirement needs, which can lead to uncertainty and potential financial stress down the road. You can take proactive steps to secure your financial future by getting a comprehensive view of your finances.

One rule of thumb that can help you manage your retirement income is the *4 percent rule*. If you withdraw 4 percent of your retirement savings in the first year after retiring and adjust that amount for inflation each subsequent year, your savings should last about thirty years. For example, if you retired with $500,000, you would withdraw $20,000 in the first year and adjust the amount for inflation in the following years. However, it's important to note that market fluctuations and changes in investment values can affect this rule, so it's always a good idea to stay informed and adapt accordingly.

To make your retirement savings last, developing an asset allocation strategy is crucial. As you approach retirement, shifting your investments from wealth-building to capital preservation and income generation is wise. This means adjusting your portfolio to include low-risk assets that can help protect your savings while generating income. There are various ways to allocate your assets, such as choosing a target-date fund that automatically adjusts your investments as you get closer to retirement, creating a two-part investment plan with a mix of stocks and bonds, or personally selecting individual stocks and bonds based on your preferences.

Another tip to extend the lifespan of your retirement savings is to consider delaying taking Social Security benefits. Depending on your birth year, you can increase your monthly benefits by waiting until your full retirement age, typically between sixty-five and sixty-seven. Taking Social Security at age sixty-two may result in a 30 percent reduction in your monthly benefits, so it's worth waiting if it aligns with your financial plan.

Additionally, working part-time during retirement can be a great way to supplement your income. It provides some financial support and keeps you engaged and active. Downsizing to a smaller home can also reduce your housing expenses, while being mindful of unnecessary costs can help you save more and make your retirement income go further.

By following these tips and working closely with a financial advisor, you can ensure that your retirement income lasts and that you enjoy a comfortable and stress-free retirement. Everyone's situation is unique, so it's important to tailor these strategies to fit your specific needs and goals.

Linsey Mills with Andrea Stephenson

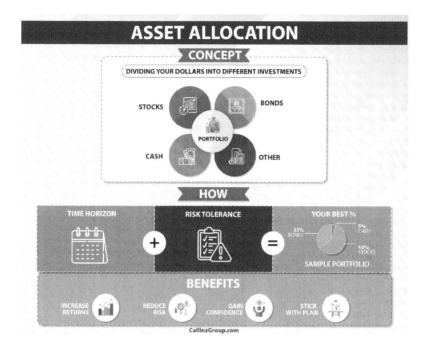

How Does Social Security Work?

Social security is a program in the US that helps people who are disabled, retired, or have lost a loved one. It's administered by the Social Security Administration, which is part of the government. Think of it as an insurance program where you and other workers contribute money through your jobs, and that money is then used to pay benefits to those who qualify.

To receive retirement benefits, you generally need to be at least sixty-two years old, and you need to have paid into the program for at least ten years. However, if you wait longer to collect your benefits, you'll receive a higher monthly amount. The actual amount you receive depends on how much you earned during your highest-earning years.

Social security isn't just for retirees. People who cannot work due to a disability and surviving spouses or children may also be eligible for benefits if they meet specific requirements. Even spouses or ex-spouses can qualify for benefits based on their partner's or former partner's earnings. Additionally, children of retirees can receive benefits until they turn eighteen (or longer if they're disabled or still in school).

Now, let's talk numbers. The amount of money you can expect from Social Security varies based on your earnings history. As of December 2022, the average monthly benefit for retired individuals was $1,688.35. But remember, the longer you wait to start collecting benefits, the more money you'll receive each month. In 2023, the maximum monthly benefit for someone who starts at age sixty-two is $2,572; for those who wait until age seventy, it's $4,555. To account for inflation, Social Security benefits are adjusted annually to keep up with the rising cost of living.

Social security also offers a special minimum benefit for people with low incomes for long periods. This minimum benefit starts at $49.40 monthly in 2023 and increases for each additional year of low-income work.

If you're curious about how much money you might receive from Social Security, you can use the calculator on the US Social Security Administration website. It'll give you an estimate based on your earnings history.

Remember, Social Security is just one part of your retirement plan. It's essential to consider other sources of income and work with a financial professional to create a comprehensive strategy that aligns with your specific needs and goals.

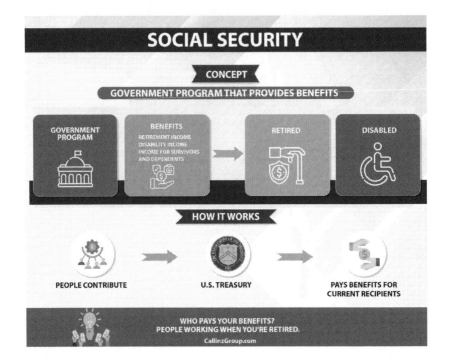

What Are Tax Considerations for Retirement?

Before you retire, it's crucial to consider taxes because the government can dip into your retirement savings, including Social Security, pensions, and 401(k)s. Even your home state may have its own set of taxes to consider. Each state has its own rules, so it's essential to check how much tax you may owe. Let's explore some key ways retirement income can be taxed.

Let's start with Social Security. While some people receiving Social Security benefits don't have to pay taxes, others may need to pay federal income tax on up to 85 percent of their benefits. It all depends on their *provisional income*, which is their income plus half of their Social Security benefits. If their provisional income falls below $25,000 (or $32,000 for married couples), their Social Security benefits are tax-free. If it's between $25,000 and $34,000 (or $32,000 and $44,000 for married couples), up to half of their benefits may be taxable. If their provisional income exceeds $34,000 (or $44,000 for married couples), up to 85 percent of their benefits could be subject to taxes.

Now let's talk about 401(k)s and traditional IRAs. These special retirement accounts allow you to contribute money and reduce the taxes you owe for that year. The money you put in can grow tax-free until you withdraw it during retirement. However, once you retire and start taking money out of these accounts, you must pay taxes on the withdrawn amount. This means you'll owe money to the government on the savings you've accumulated, including the investment returns and the untaxed portion.

Remember that you can only keep your money in these accounts for a while. You'll need to start taking required minimum distributions (RMDs) each year at a certain age. Currently, the RMD age is seventy-three for 401(k)s and traditional IRAs. However, before 2023, it used to be seventy-two. If you turned seventy-two in 2022, your first RMD is due by April 1, 2023. If you continue working past seventy-three and have a 401(k) with your current employer, you can delay RMDs until you retire, as long as you own less than 5 percent of the company.

When you withdraw money from a traditional IRA or 401(k), you must pay taxes based on your income tax rate. However, any contributions you make after paying taxes or contributions that aren't tax-deductible won't be counted as taxable income when you withdraw them. If you withdraw money before turning 59½, you'll also face a penalty and regular taxes.

Now, let's discuss Roth IRAs and Roth 401(k)s. These accounts offer significant tax benefits in the long run. While you can't deduct the money you contribute from your taxes, you won't have to pay taxes on it when you withdraw it in the future. There are a couple of things to consider: you must have had the Roth account for at least five years before withdrawing money tax-free, and if you withdraw any earnings before reaching 59½ years old, you'll be subject to a 10 percent penalty.

Roth 401(k)s follow the same principles. You won't receive a tax deduction for contributions but won't owe taxes when you withdraw the money as long as you've had the account for at least five years. The five-year period starts counting from the first time you contribute to the Roth 401(k).

Now let's touch on the taxation of stocks, bonds, and mutual funds. If you sell these investments after holding them for over a year, the money you make is taxed at a lower rate, known as the *long-term capital gains tax rate*. This rate can be 0 percent, 15 percent, or 20 percent, depending on your income level. For example, if you earned less than $41,675 in 2022, you won't owe any taxes on the profits from selling these investments. However, if you sell them before owning them for a year, you'll be taxed at your regular income tax rate. If you incur losses on your investments, you can use those losses to offset gains in other assets, up to $3,000 per year. You can also carry forward any excess losses to future years.

Dividends are another aspect to consider. If you own stocks, you may receive dividends, which are payments from the company. There are two types of dividends for tax purposes: qualified and non-qualified. *Qualified dividends* are taxed at lower rates, while *non-qualified dividends* are taxed as regular income.

When it comes to interest earned on savings accounts, CDs, or corporate bonds, you'll need to pay regular taxes on that income. However, if you invest in municipal bonds or bonds from your home state, you may be exempt from federal or state taxes on the interest. You'll be taxed at capital gains rates if you sell corporate or municipal bonds and generate a profit.

Now let's touch on taxes and pensions. When you receive money from a pension plan provided by your employer or the government, you have to pay taxes on it as regular income. The exact amount you owe depends on your income tax rate. If you didn't contribute after-tax money to the pension plan, you'll need to pay taxes on the entire amount you receive.

Lastly, let's address the taxation of home sales. When you sell your primary home and make a profit, the government may take a portion of that money as taxes. However, if you've lived in the house as your primary residence for at least two of the past five years, you might not have to pay taxes on up to $250,000 of the profit (or $500,000 for married couples). If your profit exceeds those limits, you'll be subject to a special lower tax rate. Unfortunately, you can't claim a tax deduction if you sell your home for less than what you paid.

Tax laws can change over time, so staying informed and consulting with a tax professional is crucial for personalized advice and guidance tailored to your situation. Understanding how taxes impact your retirement income allows you to plan more effectively and make informed decisions to minimize your tax burden.

What Are Healthcare Considerations for Retirement?

When you're thinking about retirement, it's essential not to overlook the cost of healthcare. Even with Medicare, there are still deductibles and copays to consider. A couple retiring at age sixty-five might need as much as $325,000 in savings for healthcare expenses. It may sound daunting, but the good news is that you can plan for these costs.

While healthcare expenses stay relatively consistent for most years, they increase as you get older. Healthcare costs are projected to double in the first twenty years of retirement. Our healthcare needs often increase as we age, while other expenses like entertainment and travel tend to decrease.

Several factors can influence how much healthcare will cost in retirement. Your health status plays a significant role. If you smoke, have chronic health conditions, or frequently visit the doctor, you should anticipate higher healthcare expenses. On the other hand, if you're in good health, don't smoke, and rarely need medical attention, your costs may be lower.

Location is another factor to consider. Healthcare prices can vary depending on where you live. While traditional Medicare coverage remains the same nationwide, other types, like prescription coverage and Medicare Advantage plans, can differ from one place to another.

The age at which you retire also affects your healthcare costs. Retiring before age sixty-five means you'll need alternative coverage until you become eligible for Medicare. Options include the following:

- Staying on your spouse's plan

- Using COBRA coverage
- Purchasing insurance on the open market or through a professional association

The choices you make regarding your healthcare plans can have an impact as well. When enrolling in Medicare, you must decide between traditional Medicare or Medicare Advantage. Additionally, you may need to consider adding Medigap coverage, prescription coverage, and coverage for dental and vision expenses.

Long-term care insurance is another critical consideration. Medicare typically doesn't cover nursing homes, assisted living facilities, or in-home care costs. Long-term care insurance can help protect your retirement savings by covering these expenses.

There are options available to help cover healthcare costs in retirement. Health Savings Accounts (HSAs) are one such option. You can contribute to an HSA before transitioning to Medicare if you have a high-deductible health plan. Contributions to an HSA are tax-free, and the funds can be used for medical expenses not covered by Medicare, such as dental treatments, doctor visits, and prescription drugs. HSAs can be a valuable tool for saving for medical expenses if you have a high-deductible health plan before transitioning to Medicare.

Medicare itself is another option to consider. It is a government-provided health insurance program for individuals aged sixty-five and older. However, it's essential to understand that Medicare doesn't cover all medical costs. You will still have out-of-pocket expenses like deductibles and copays. Understanding what

Medicare does and doesn't cover will help you plan for healthcare expenses in retirement.

For instance, Medicare does not cover long-term care, which is necessary if you require extended assistance with daily activities due to illness or injury. The costs associated with long-term care can be substantial, with even a month's stay in a nursing home costing nearly $8,000. Long-term care insurance can help cover these expenses and protect your retirement savings.

When planning for retirement and considering healthcare options, seeking expert advice is crucial. Professionals can guide you in understanding your choices and making the best decisions for your circumstances. Don't wait until it's too late—start planning early to safeguard your future.

Remember, healthcare costs are a crucial factor to consider in retirement planning. By being proactive and taking the necessary steps, you can ensure that you're financially prepared for your healthcare needs during retirement.

SECTION 7

Giving

The legacy of the life you live will be determined by the Time, Talent, Treasure and Testimony you give.

~ Linsey Mills

Why Is Giving Important?

Giving is genuinely inspiring and profoundly impacts both the giver and the recipient. It's a powerful act that can ignite a chain reaction of generosity. When we witness others being generous, it stirs something within us and motivates us to give. Not only do those who give back experience immense happiness, but they also lead more meaningful and fulfilling lives. Allow me to delve into the reasons why giving is so important.

You might wonder why we should bother giving when discussing money matters. Focusing on topics like paying off debt, budgeting, and building wealth is understandable, as they seem more productive. Some might question why they should work hard to accumulate wealth only to give it away.

The truth is that giving back brings peace and happiness. Clinging onto everything and believing that a larger bank account will shield us from trouble is a recipe for eternal dissatisfaction. The pursuit of acquiring more wealth and possessions is an insatiable endeavor. However, giving generously makes us realize that true financial security isn't derived from accumulating more money and material possessions. Genuine financial freedom stems from having the freedom to live and give to others.

Now, let's explore the benefits of giving back:

1. Increased happiness and reduced stress: People who give to others tend to be happier and experience less stress. This is because acts of giving stimulate the release of oxytocin, a chemical in our brains associated with happiness and well-being. As the famous saying goes, "It is better to give than to receive."

2. Enhanced health: Giving back can improve health by instilling a sense of purpose and motivation to adopt a healthier lifestyle. When we engage in acts of generosity, we feel a deeper connection to our well-being and the well-being of others.

3. Expanded network: Giving provides opportunities to connect with like-minded individuals and expand our social and professional networks. We meet people who share similar values and passions through volunteering or contributing to charitable organizations, creating meaningful connections.

4. Community awareness: Engaging in acts of giving allows us to better understand the challenges and needs within our community. It opens our eyes to the issues others face and empowers us to make a positive impact locally.

5. Unleashed potential: Giving back allows us to utilize and share our unique skills and talents. By offering our

expertise, we can help others overcome obstacles, inspire growth, and create a better future.

6. Broadened perspective: Through giving, we gain new perspectives on life and develop empathy for others. It allows us to step outside our circumstances and understand the struggles and triumphs of those around us.

7. Personal growth: Engaging in acts of giving fosters personal growth. It challenges us to step out of our comfort zones, develop new skills, and overcome obstacles. The experience of giving can transform us into more compassionate, resilient, and confident individuals.

8. Acquired knowledge: When we give back, we learn about different issues, causes, and organizations. This knowledge enriches our understanding of the world and equips us to make informed decisions about where and how to contribute.

9. Boosted self-esteem: Giving back reinforces our sense of self-worth and significance. Knowing that we have positively impacted someone's life boosts our self-esteem and reinforces our belief in our ability to make a difference.

Now that you understand the importance of giving, you might be wondering how to get started. Here are five ways to make a difference:

1. Donate to organizations: Consider allocating a portion of your income, such as 10 percent, to support charitable organizations that align with your values and the causes

you care about. There are countless nonprofits making a difference, so find one that resonates with you.

2. Assist individuals or families: If you know someone in need, providing financial support can profoundly impact their lives. Even a small contribution can bring about positive change and improve their circumstances.

3. Volunteer your time: Giving isn't limited to money alone; you can also give your time. Engage in community service, lend a helping hand, or offer your skills and knowledge to organizations or individuals in need. You don't need vast resources or copious amounts of free time; a genuine desire to make a difference is all it takes.

4. Share your talents: Everyone possesses unique skills and talents. Identify ways to utilize your abilities to bring joy and value to others. Whether knitting warm scarves for the homeless or providing free tutoring to underprivileged students, your talents can make a meaningful difference in someone's life.

5. Give unwanted items: Decluttering your possessions can also be a form of giving. Donate clothes, furniture, or even food to individuals or organizations that can benefit from them. Your unused items can bring comfort and support to those in need.

Giving back is essential because it cultivates true financial peace, happiness, and fulfillment—the amount you give matters less than taking that first step. Whether you give your money, time, talent, or unused belongings, your impact on someone's life can be immeasurable. Embrace the power of giving and experience the profound joy it brings you and others.

What Are the Different Types of Giving Models?

Let's talk about different types of giving that you can consider when supporting nonprofit organizations and charities. Each type of donation plays a crucial role in helping these groups fulfill their mission and make a positive impact. Here are nine common types of donations:

1. One-time donations: This is the most common type of donation, where you give an organization a specific amount of money in a single instance. You can make these donations online, by phone, by mail, or in person.

2. Recurring donations: With recurring donations, you set up automated, regular contributions to an organization. This is a convenient option where you decide on an amount and frequency for your donations.

3. Planned donations: Planned giving, or legacy giving, involves including significant gifts in your financial or estate plans. These gifts can be bequests, charitable trust payments, life insurance policies, or retirement fund contributions.

4. Tribute or memorial donations: People often make donations to honor or remember loved ones. Organizations may offer donors the opportunity to make tribute or memorial contributions, which can be done through specific campaigns or general donation forms. For example, you may make tribute gifts on special occasions like Father's Day or Mother's Day.

5. Stock donations: Instead of giving cash, some donors donate stocks, bonds, or other securities to organizations.

6. In-kind donations: In-kind donations involve non-monetary items or services. This could include donating office supplies, offering free professional services like accounting or legal assistance, or providing goods for an organization's specific needs. In-kind donations can help reduce expenses for the organization and allow them to allocate resources to other areas.

7. Matching donations: Matching donations occur when a donor agrees to match the contributions made by others up to a certain amount. For instance, a donor may commit to matching donations up to $1,000, so any contributions made to the organization up to that limit will be matched. This can serve as a powerful incentive for more people to give and increase the overall impact of their donations.

8. Workplace donations: Many workplaces offer programs that enable employees to donate to nonprofits or charities through payroll deductions. Check with your HR department or manager to find out if your workplace offers this opportunity to support causes you care about.

These are just some of the different types of giving you can explore. Remember that each type of donation, regardless of the amount or form, contributes to making a positive difference in the lives of others and supports the valuable work carried out by nonprofit organizations and charities.

Giving Circles Are Becoming Popular. What Are They?

A *giving circle* is a powerful concept that has gained popularity in recent years. A giving circle is a group of individuals who come together to pool their money and resources to support charitable causes. It's like a team effort to positively impact the world!

One of the great things about giving circles is that they offer a collaborative and democratic approach to philanthropy. Members of the circle work together to decide where their collective funds should go. This involves discussions, presentations, and votes to determine which organizations or projects will receive their support. This is a way to make decisions as a group and ensure everyone's voices are heard.

Another remarkable aspect of giving circles is the sense of community they create. When you join a giving circle, you connect with like-minded individuals who share your values and goals. You get to meet regularly, talk about philanthropy, learn about different organizations, and share your experiences with giving. It's a chance to build relationships and surround yourself with people passionate about making a difference.

Giving circles also offer flexibility. You can tailor the circle to focus on a specific cause or issue you care deeply about. Or you can support various organizations and projects depending on the group's interests. The key is finding a setup that works best for you and your circle members.

The impact of giving circles can be quite remarkable. By pooling their resources, circle members can amplify their contributions and make a more significant difference. Even if each member gives a small amount, when combined, it can substantially impact the organizations they support and the communities they serve.

Let me give you some examples to illustrate how giving circles have made a difference. The Birmingham Change Fund is a giving circle of African American professionals who pooled their, time talent and treasures together to make grants in the Birmingham community. Their three focus areas are education, economics and health care. Another great example is SPIN (Sisterhood of Philanthropists Impacting Needs) is a philanthropic giving circle of Black women in the Denver community who leverage their collective strengths to positively impact marginalized women and adolescent girls.

Giving circles are especially beneficial for young people who may have a limited amount of money to donate individually. By joining a giving circle, they can pool their resources with others and have a more significant impact. It's a fantastic way for young people to learn about different organizations and causes while actively participating in philanthropy.

If you're interested in starting your giving circle with family, friends, or classmates, here are a few tips to get you started:

1. Find a cause or issue that you and your group are passionate about. It could be anything from animal welfare and environmental sustainability to social justice.

2. Set a fundraising goal to give your efforts direction and motivation.

3. Identify potential partners who are interested in joining your giving circle. Reach out to friends, family members, or

anyone else who shares your passion for making a difference.

4. Decide on a donation amount that works for everyone in the group. It could be a small monthly contribution, a one-time donation, or a combination of both.

5. Research organizations that are working on the cause you care about. Look for groups with a track record of success, a clear mission and vision, and transparent operations.

6. Make a plan for how to distribute your funds. You can have discussions or voting processes or even invite representatives from organizations to present their work to the group.

7. Finally, celebrate your success as a group when you reach your fundraising goal and distribute your funds. This is a chance to reflect on the impact you've made and build a sense of camaraderie among your giving circle members.

Giving circles are a fantastic way to engage in philanthropy, build relationships, and make a meaningful impact.

What Are the Tax Implications of Charitable Giving?

Now let's talk about the tax implications of charitable giving! It's important to understand how your donations can affect your taxes, so let's go over some key points.

First, it's worth noting that seeking advice from a tax professional before making significant charitable donations is always a good idea. They can provide personalized guidance based on your specific situation.

Here are a few important things to keep in mind:

1. Receipts for donations: If you donate $250 or more to a single charity, make sure to request a receipt. Even if you give cash, you'll need a receipt or a record from your bank, regardless of the donation amount.

2. Appraisals for high-value items: If you donate items worth over $5,000, you'll typically need to obtain an independent, written appraisal of their value.

3. Deducting value of received items: If you receive something in return for your donation, such as a book or a meal at a charity event, you'll need to subtract the fair market value of that item from your donation before claiming it as a tax deduction.

4. Itemizing deductions: To benefit from tax deductions related to charitable giving, you'll need to itemize your deductions on your tax return. By itemizing, you'll be able to claim your contributions and potentially lower your tax bill.

There are limits on the amount you can deduct each year for various types of donations. If you plan to give a substantial amount, it's advisable to consult with a tax professional who can provide guidance based on your specific circumstances.

Let's take a look at the tax implications of different types of gifts:

1. Cash donations: When making cash donations, it's important to obtain a receipt from the charity or keep a record from your bank as proof of your contribution.

2. Volunteer expenses: While you can't deduct the value of your time volunteering, you can deduct transportation costs and other expenses related to your volunteer work.

3. Non-cash donations: You can donate various items provided they are in good condition. If the donated item does not align with the mission of the charity, you can generally deduct either the amount you paid for it or its current value, whichever is less. However, if the item is relevant to the charity's mission, you can deduct its current value.

4. Donations of appreciated assets: Donating something you made or an item that would have generated income if sold might limit your deduction. On the other hand, if you donate an asset that has increased in value and you've owned it for more than a year, you can deduct its full current value without paying taxes on the capital gain.

5. Property with depreciated value: If you donate property that has gone down in value, your deduction may be further limited to its current value.

6. Stocks and investments: Donating stocks or other investments with increased value can provide additional tax advantages. For instance, if you want to give $100,000 worth of stock to a charity, donating the stock directly allows you to deduct the total value without paying taxes on the gain.

7. Selling depreciated stocks: If you own stocks that have lost value, it might be more beneficial to sell them first, utilize

the loss to lower your taxes, and then donate the remaining money.

There are specific strategies you can employ to simplify the giving process and maximize tax benefits. For example, using a *donor-advised fund* allows you to donate stocks and receive an immediate tax break. You can then distribute the funds to various charities over time, and any remaining money can grow and be donated later.

If you wish to donate assets to a charity but still receive income for a specific period, options like a *charitable remainder trust* or a *pooled income fund* can be beneficial. Additionally, individuals over 70 ½ years old can donate money directly from their IRA to a charity without incurring taxes, although it's important to note that this type of donation does not provide a tax deduction.

Remember, while tax benefits are an added bonus, the primary focus should be on supporting the organizations you care about. Consider consulting a financial planner or tax advisor to help determine the best donation method for your specific needs and goals.

How Do You Budget for Giving?

Donating money to a good cause is an excellent financial goal that helps those in need and brings a sense of fulfillment and happiness to yourself. It's a meaningful way to make a positive impact and redistribute some of your resources to those who are less fortunate. However, it is important to budget for giving, so you can ensure you put aside the money you want to give.

Incorporating donations into your budget may require adjustments and careful consideration of your current spending habits. Here are a few steps you can take:

1. Determine your donation amount: Start by deciding how much you want to give each month. Set a realistic amount that aligns with your financial situation and goals. If you cannot initially donate as much as you'd like, that's okay. As your financial circumstances improve, you can always work your way up over time.

2. Budgeting strategies: You can consider two popular budgeting strategies: the *50/30/20 rule* and the *one-number approach*. The 50/30/20 rule suggests dividing your income into three categories: 50 percent for needs, 30 percent for wants/enjoyment, and 20 percent for savings or future goals. You can adjust these percentages to fit your priorities, including allocating a portion for donations. On the other hand, the one-number approach simplifies things by assigning a specific amount you can spend each week after deducting fixed expenses like rent. You must factor that into your weekly spending amount if you make monthly donations.

3. Strategies for taking action: To turn your commitment to donate into action, consider the following strategies:

- Align with causes that excite you: Choose organizations or initiatives that resonate deeply with your values and interests. This way, your donations will have a more meaningful impact on the causes you care about.

- Set up recurring donations: By setting up automatic monthly contributions, you can make your donations more consistent and ensure they happen without relying on manual reminders. It's beneficial for both the organization and you, and you'll receive donation receipts as a reminder of your commitment.

- Keep donation money separate: Consider keeping your donation money separate from your regular spending accounts. This can help you stay organized and keep track of your giving specifically. It also allows you to see the impact you're making more clearly.

- Time contributions strategically: Be mindful of the timing of your donations. For example, some organizations may have matching programs or fundraising events during specific periods, which can increase the impact of your contributions.

Remember, the goal is to find a balance between your giving aspirations and your overall financial well-being. If you ever feel overwhelmed or uncertain about budgeting for giving, seeking guidance from a financial planner or advisor can provide valuable insights tailored to your unique situation.

By incorporating donations into your budget and taking practical steps to make giving a regular practice, you'll make a positive difference in the world and experience the joy and fulfillment that come from helping others.

SECTION 8

Teaching Financial Literacy to Kids

A child's financial lessons aren't taught. They are experienced through the actions of the parents.

~Linsey Mills

Why Is It Important to Teach Kids about Money?

Teaching kids about money is a fantastic idea to help them develop critical financial skills. Let me share some practical tips and activities that can make learning about money a fun and engaging experience for your little one.

To start, let's focus on the basics. It's essential to introduce your child to the different types of money, like coins and bills, and teach them how to count them. It can be challenging for young kids, but we can make it enjoyable with exciting activities.

One activity you can try is a coin comparison game. Gather a penny, nickel, dime, and quarter and place them on a table. Take the time to introduce each coin's name, starting with the penny. You can also point out their colors and the smoothness of their edges. Grab a magnifying glass and compare the coins, discussing their similarities and differences to make it even more enjoyable.

Now, let's create a pretend grocery store! Collect some used boxes, cans, and bags, and label them with prices representing each coin's value. Give your child some real money and let them pretend to shop for items. They can also put treats and toys in boxes marked with different coin values. This way, they practice buying things using a handful of coins. Remember to reinforce the values and emphasize that a coin's size doesn't determine its worth.

Another exciting method is to become a coin detective! Hide several coins of various values around a room and have your child search for specific ones. You can even encourage them to make coin rubbings by placing a coin under a white sheet of paper and using an unwrapped crayon to rub over it. They can write the coin's name and value next to the rubbing they created. This activity adds an interactive element to learning coin identification.

Here's a clever idea that combines money and chores. Assign different coin amounts to specific tasks and pay your child for their work. For example, taking out the trash could earn one coin, while setting the table could earn more. Over time, they'll realize that different coins have different values and that working can help them earn money. It's a great way to teach the connection between effort and financial rewards.

These activities should provide a solid foundation for your child's understanding of money. Remember, the key is to keep it fun and engaging. And if you're looking for more financial literacy activities for kids, I highly recommend checking out our book *Teach Your Child about Money Through Play*. It's filled with over 110+ games, activities, tips, and resources designed to teach kids about financial literacy from an early age.

I hope these tips and activities help you and your child embark on an exciting journey toward financial literacy.

How Can I Teach My Child to Count Money?

Teaching your child to count money is an essential skill that will set them up for financial success in the future. I'll provide some practical tips and activities to make learning to count money fun and engaging for your little one.

One fundamental principle in counting money is skip-counting. If your child hasn't mastered this skill yet, it might take some time for them to catch on, so be patient. Since our currency is based on one hundred, your child must learn how to count by fives, tens, and fifties, up to one hundred. Practice this regularly to ensure they become confident in skip-counting.

Let's explore some enjoyable activities for counting money:

1. Songs about money: Introduce your child to riddles or songs about each coin and dollar. This can help them remember what each one looks like and its value. You can find lyrics online, or if you're feeling creative, make up your own! Make it a daily routine to recite these songs or riddles with your child, and consider using visual aids like anchor charts.

2. Classifying and sorting: Once your child has a grasp of skip-counting and can identify the characteristics of each coin, it's time to practice sorting money. You can use real coins or replica play money for this activity. Have them sort the coins based on color and size. Pennies are usually easier to sort due to their copper color, but your child might need some guidance with nickels, dimes, and quarters, as they all have a similar silver color. Help them differentiate these coins by size and appearance.

3. One coin at a time: Take the time to focus on one coin at a time. Allow your child to learn at their own pace without rushing them. Start with the penny and spend as much time as they need to grasp its attributes. Discuss the coin's color, the design on its head and tail, and its value. Then, practice counting with pennies. Gradually, show them how many pennies make a dollar. Once they understand this concept, you can move on to nickels, dimes, and quarters, repeating the same process.

4. Mixing coins: After your child has practiced skip-counting, identifying coins, and understanding their values, they should be ready to count different coins together. In this step, teaching them to count from the highest value to the lowest is essential. Start with quarters, then dimes, nickels, and pennies. To avoid overwhelming them, start with a small number of mixed coins. Once you feel they're ready, you can gradually add more types of coins.

5. Financial transactions during meals or in stores: When you're at a restaurant or store with a cashier, give your child cash to make their purchase. Ensure they have more money than the cost of the meal or item. Let them approach the counter independently and interact with the cashier by ordering, paying, receiving change, and checking if they got what they ordered. This real-life experience will reinforce their understanding of money and its practical use.

To prepare your child for making their purchase, here are a few tips:

- Discuss what they want to order and ensure they know the total cost.
- Ask them how many dollars they need to buy their meal or item.
- Remind them to wait for their change after giving money to the cashier.
- You can even do a practice run where your child tells you what they plan to order.

Remember, the key is to make the learning process enjoyable and relatable. Incorporating these activities into your child's routine will help them build a strong foundation in counting money.

How Do I Teach My Children the Difference between Needs and Wants?

Teaching children the difference between needs and wants regarding money is a valuable lesson that will serve them well in the long run. It can be challenging, but I have some engaging strategies to help.

Children struggle with this concept because they're still learning how to regulate their emotions, especially when it comes to delayed gratification. Everything can feel like a need to them. It's essential to be patient and understanding during this phase.

Another factor that can contribute to confusion is the way adults use language. Sometimes we say we "need" something when it's actually a want. Children tend to mimic the words they hear, so being mindful of our language can help clear any misunderstandings.

Children also often don't make purchasing decisions for their needs. As parents, we provide them with the essentials like food, housing, and utilities. Since they don't have to make choices about these things, their needs can blend with their desires and become higher-priority wants.

So how can we teach children about needs and wants? One approach is to incorporate the vocabulary into everyday situations. When getting ready to leave the house, ask your child what they need to bring and discuss the consequences of leaving certain things behind. This helps them understand what is truly necessary for their well-being.

Another fun activity is baking. Ask your child which ingredients are essential for a successful cake and which are just extras. Flour is needed, but sprinkles are optional. By using tangible examples like this, children can start to differentiate between needs and wants.

When your child expresses a strong desire for a new toy or gadget, it's imperative to address it. Validate their feelings and acknowledge why they may want it. However, setting firm boundaries and explaining that not every want can be fulfilled is equally important. This teaches them that there are spending limits and helps manage their expectations.

Involving children in the family's budgeting process is a great practice. Explain what the family's needs are and how they are prioritized. Once the needs are met, you can discuss the amount of money available for discretionary items or "wants." This helps children understand that there's a finite amount of money and that choices must be made.

Remember, teaching the difference between needs and wants takes time and repetition. Be patient, and use everyday situations as teachable moments. Doing so will help your children develop a solid foundation for making wise financial decisions.

How Can I Teach My Kids about Earning Money?

Now I'd like to help you teach your kids about earning money in an educational and fun way. Understanding how money is earned is an essential lesson for children, and it sets the foundation for their financial future. So let's dive in!

First, explain to your kids that people can earn money in three ways. First, there's the option of working a job as an employee. When a company hires someone to perform a task, they receive a paycheck. Some jobs may require additional education, like college or trade school, to qualify for specific positions.

The second way people earn money is through owning a business. Business owners hire employees to make or sell products or provide services. They can make money through passive income, where the company generates money whether they work or not, or through portfolio income, where they buy items at a lower price and sell them for a higher price.

Lastly, individuals can earn money by being investors. This involves buying items that increase in value over time, such as real estate or businesses, which can generate additional income.

Now that your kids understand how money can be earned, let's explore some practical ways to teach them firsthand.

1. Doing chores: Many families already have a system where kids are responsible for household chores. You can take it a step further by offering them extra chores they can do for money. Cleaning the dishes or walking the dog could earn them some extra cash, teaching them that work equals money.

2. Yard work: Encourage your kids to ask neighbors if they need help with yard work. This is an excellent opportunity for them to learn how to actively seek work and understand the value of their time and effort.

3. Selling toys: If your child has toys they no longer use, they can sell them and earn some money. This teaches them about being frugal and introduces the idea of reducing, reusing, and recycling.

4. Crafting: Kids can tap into their creativity by making and selling things on platforms like Etsy. This hands-on experience helps them understand the basics of running a business and nurtures their entrepreneurial spirit.

5. Pet sitting: Older kids can earn money by pet sitting or walking dogs for neighbors or friends. This opportunity allows them to negotiate pay, communicate with people of all ages, and take responsibility for the well-being of animals. These skills contribute to their independence and savviness with money.

You're equipping children with crucial life skills by teaching them about money and how to manage it wisely. Instilling good financial habits is never too early, as they'll lay the groundwork for a successful financial future. So have fun with these activities and watch your kids thrive as they learn the value of earning and managing money!

How Do I Teach My Child about Saving Money?

Teaching your child about saving money is a wonderful way to instill financial responsibility from an early age. Kids are often drawn to spending, so it's important to guide them down the path to saving too. Let's explore some strategies to help your child learn about saving money in a fun and effective way!

Giving your child pocket money is an excellent way to empower them and allow them to take charge of their money. Consistency is key here, as it allows them to budget and work toward their savings goals. While it's great to let them earn extra cash for chores, explaining that specific household tasks should be done to contribute to the family, not just for money, is essential.

Open and ongoing conversations about money are crucial. Take the time to explain why you work, what earning money means, and the costs of different things. You can even introduce the concept of investing by mentioning that you own shares, known as stocks, in some of the companies you shop from regularly. When your child wants to buy something, discuss with them what they did to earn money, what they'll have left after the purchase, and other ways to earn additional funds.

Leveraging technology can also be a valuable teaching tool. Some apps like GoHenry and Rooster Money allow children to track their balances and learn about spending, saving, giving, and even growing their money. Allowing your child to make small mistakes with money while they're young is better than letting them making big ones when they're older and facing more significant financial decisions.

Another effective method is letting your child observe your saving habits. Show them how you transfer money into a savings account or collect coins in a jar. They can witness the process and understand where the money goes. Remember to set a positive example by practicing good financial habits, such as budgeting and regularly reviewing your finances.

To help your child get started with saving money, here are some simple steps you can encourage:

- Teach them to distinguish between wants and needs by showing them the difference between essentials like food and clothing and extras like designer sneakers or the latest smartphone.
- Allow them to earn their own money by offering an allowance for completed chores.
- Help them define a savings goal and break it down into manageable steps.
- Provide a designated place for them to save money, whether it's a piggy bank, a bank account, or a kid-friendly debit card.
- Encourage them to track their spending, understand where their money goes, and adjust to reach their savings goals.
- Consider offering incentives to motivate them, such as matching a percentage of what they save or giving them a bonus for reaching specific savings milestones.
- Allow them to make mistakes and learn from them, as it's an integral part of the learning process.

- Play the role of a lender to teach the valuable lesson that saving involves delayed gratification and that waiting can sometimes result in lower costs.
- Keep the conversation about money going by discussing it regularly and helping them learn about the importance of saving.

Setting a good example is vital, so be a saver yourself and involve the whole family in saving for something together, like a family vacation or a new computer.

By implementing these strategies and fostering a positive saving mindset, you're equipping your child with essential financial skills that will benefit them throughout their lives.

What Should I Tell My Child about Debt?

When talking to your child about debt, providing them with a holistic perspective is important. Let's dive into this topic together and explore different viewpoints. At the end, I'll share my opinion.

So what exactly is debt? *Debt* is a promise to pay back borrowed money. For example, imagine a girl named Jackie who needed a $200 loan from the bank to start her business. The bank provided her with $200, but they required her to pay back $225. That extra $25 is called *interest*, the cost of borrowing money. That is how the bank makes money.

Now, it's worth noting that many people don't like being in debt. Owing money to someone can cause stress and frustration, especially when bills start piling up. Sometimes, people spend more money on interest payments than the actual debt, also known as the *principal*.

Our co-author, Andrea, shares her personal experience with you: "When I was in my twenties, my biggest debt was my student loans from college. At one point, I owed over $30,000. Every time I received my bill, I noticed that the interest number decreased, but the principal or debt number remained the same. This was because I was paying the minimum amount to avoid late fees. It took me twelve years to pay it off, and I only saw the principal decrease when I started paying more than the minimum amount."

So instead of incurring debt, some people save until they can afford what they want. Although it may take longer, it brings them peace of mind and freedom from owing money. Some people even take on extra jobs to accelerate the saving process. Additionally, organizations like churches and non-profits may ask for donations to fund community-building initiatives or purchase necessary resources.

However, some individuals want stuff immediately but must borrow money to pay for it. They often turn to credit cards for instant gratification. A credit card allows you to borrow money up to a specific limit, with the understanding that you'll repay the bank with interest. When applying for a credit card, the bank reviews your credit reports to assess your ability to repay the debt. The bank is more likely to approve your application if you have a good credit score (700 and above).

It's essential to know the annual percentage rate (APR) and the due date for your monthly credit card bill. The APR represents the interest charged for borrowing money through your credit card. Late payments can result in additional fees and an increase in your interest rate, leading to paying more than what you borrowed.

One common challenge with credit cards is overspending, which means spending more money than you can afford. This often leads to mounting bills and debt that can be difficult to repay. Overspending can happen for various reasons, such as wanting to appear wealthier by purchasing luxury items, not wanting to go without desired items like eating out, being addicted to shopping, or simply lacking a household budget that tracks expenses.

Now let's discuss the difference between good debt and bad debt. Some people see debt as a tool to acquire assets. Our previous conversations explored the distinction between *assets* (things that generate income) and *liabilities* (things that drain your finances). This concept applies to debt as well. *Good debt* refers to borrowing money to buy assets like real estate or a business. However, it's crucial to thoroughly assess the potential income-generating capacity of these assets before taking on debt. For example, when starting a business, you need to ensure there is demand for your product or service. Regarding real estate, you want to be sure that rental income will cover expenses and provide a profit.

Here's my opinion: I strongly recommend avoiding debt whenever possible. It's always best to save money before starting a business or investing in real estate. By doing so, you won't have to worry about interest payments or the stress of owing money to someone else.

Remember, this is a complex topic, and opinions can vary. Exploring different perspectives and making informed decisions based on your financial situation and goals is essential.

What Are Some Everyday Kid-Friendly Financial Literacy Experiences?

A Little Note from Andrea:

Now let's chat about real-world, kid-friendly experiences that can help teach financial literacy. It's always great when children can learn through hands-on experiences, right? Field trips are perfect for this! They give kids a chance to see how things work in the real world and make connections to what they learn at school or home. Plus, they encourage problem-solving and let children have a direct impact.

In this section, we will focus on financial literacy field trips. These trips are fantastic because they can help your child understand how money works, circulates, and is used for transactions. The best part is you can plan these activities with your child whenever you have the time, and it's a fun way to dive deep into the world of money.

As a financial consultant and someone who creates interactive financial education experiences, I've seen firsthand how powerful it is for children to experience financial concepts and strategies themselves. And guess what? You don't have to be a financial expert to start teaching your kids about money. In fact, you are your child's very first financial advisor and educator. The financial transactions they see you make can greatly impact their financial future.

A great way to teach your child about money is to look for opportunities in your everyday routines to engage them in financial and business transactions. Here are a few examples that can create lasting memories. Some of these experiences even stuck with us from our childhoods!

Financial Transactions at Meals

Imagine this: You're at a restaurant, and there's a cashier. When you order your meal, why not give your child some cash to make their purchase? Make sure they have more money than the cost of the meal. Then, let them go to the counter and interact with the cashier. They can order their meal, give the cashier the cash, receive their change, and check if they got what they ordered. It's a fantastic way to involve them in a financial transaction and practice their skills.

To get your child prepared for this experience, you can have a little chat beforehand. Talk about what they want to order and make sure they know the total cost of their meal, including any extras like a drink or dessert. Ask them how many dollars they'll need to buy everything. Remind them to wait for their change after giving the money to the cashier. You can even do a practice run at home where they tell you what they plan to order.

See how easy it is to create these memorable experiences? They're fun and valuable for teaching your child about money.

Financial Life Lessons and Teachable Moments

Let's talk about some financial life lessons and teachable moments that can impact your child's understanding of money. Sometimes, a situation may arise where your child doesn't receive the correct change when paying for an item. In that case, you can discuss the correct change that should have been given to your child. Then, encourage them to return to the counter and politely inform the cashier about the mistake, asking for the correct amount. You need to be there to support your child and let them take the lead in talking to the cashier to resolve the issue.

You and your child might feel slightly nervous during the first few transactions. Still, with practice, your child will become more confident in communicating with adults and handling everyday financial transactions. It's all about building their skills and independence.

Here's another scenario you can try: Set a spending limit for your child and let them decide which items they can afford with the money you've given them. For example, they might have to choose the complimentary cup of water instead of buying a non-free drink to stay within their budget. It's a great way to teach them about making choices based on their financial resources.

These suggestions can be used with your students or children, creating valuable financial life lessons and teachable moments. Keep the learning going!

Financial Life Lessons and Teachable Moments at the Bank

Now, let's move on to financial transactions at financial institutions. The next time you visit the bank, why not let your child take charge of making a deposit or withdrawal with the teller? Instruct them to communicate their request to the teller, whether a deposit or withdrawal from their checking or savings account. They'll be thrilled to see your little financial guru in action as the teller processes the transaction and hands over the receipt. Remind your child that the teller might ask, "Is there anything else I can help you with today?" Encourage them to respond to the teller's question and, of course, say thank you.

Financial life lessons and teachable moments can also happen at the bank when you take your child to open a custodial bank account. Take the opportunity to explain to your child what it means to have their own account and the significance of this step. Let them actively participate in making deposits and withdrawals, as appropriate, regularly. This will help them develop confidence and a sense of responsibility when dealing with financial professionals.

As a parent, teacher, or guardian, always look for opportunities to turn everyday activities into educational experiences that enhance your child's financial literacy. Don't let your child be a passive participant in life. Start building their financial and business decision-making skills from an early age.

Here are a few tips to make the banking field trip more meaningful:

- Take the time to point out and explain the roles of bank employees, such as tellers, bank managers, and customer service representatives.

- If there's enough time, encourage your child to ask the employees to explain their roles. This can be a valuable learning experience for them.

Financial Trip to Pay Bills

As a child, I remember paying bills with my mom monthly. I would sit at the kitchen table or in the car, look at the utility bills, and write checks to pay them. My mom would sign them and explain to me the purpose of each bill. We would go into each building where the bill was due and pay it. Sometimes, but rarely, she would mail the payment off. I think it made her feel better to deliver the payment herself. It gave me a better appreciation of how my parents provided for us.

You can do this same activity with your child. Instruct your child to write checks and money orders when they see separate bills for the lights, gas, water, trash pickup, and other household expenses. If you pay your bills online, have them participate in this process. Other bills your child can observe you pay are as follows:

- Mortgage payment: Explain how the bank helps you pay for your house by loaning you money. Don't forget to discuss how you must repay the debt to the bank with interest included. Also show your child the mortgage bill and where the interest and principal amounts are located.
- Credit card bill: Explain the purpose of a credit card. Credit cards help you purchase items faster. Review that a credit card is a debt that must be repaid with interest.
- Cable and internet bills: Explain that cable and internet provide entertainment for the family. However, many people use high-speed internet for work. If you have other purposes for having cable and the internet, explain that as well. Review the services you are paying for and the bill amount.

- Cell phone bills: Explain that cell phones help you communicate with others and research information (if you have a smartphone). Many people use cell phones for work. Explain the cell phone company's services, like texting and high-speed internet. Also review the bill amount.

Please note:

1. In all your bills, pinpoint the taxes you pay.
2. Review with your child what taxes pay for, such as roads, schools, and healthcare.
3. Discuss the due dates and what happens if you pay a bill late.

Financial Trip to the Grocery Store

Many of us go to the grocery weekly or biweekly because we need food. Why not create a robust financial literacy lesson from this?

Let your child plan the meal for the day:

1. They should think about what the family likes to eat. They can interview family members and make a list.
2. Have them come up with estimated costs for each item by looking online or in the newspaper. Help your child determine the total estimated cost for their items.
3. Go shopping with your child to purchase the items.

If possible, allow your child to conduct the transaction with the grocery cashier and have them count their change. You may also allow them to scan the food in the self-checkout aisle. Remember to keep the receipt. When you get home, prepare the meals and make a list of what the items cost.

More tips for going to the grocery store:

- Take a calculator to keep track of the costs as you put the groceries in your shopping cart.
- Discuss with your child how you compare which brand or category of specific items you buy. For example, do you buy organic fruit? Why or why not?

Financial Trip for a Major Purchase

A major purchase includes buying a more expensive item such as a car, television, oven, computer, furniture, or washer or dryer. When you are buying these types of products, take your children along to observe the process. They will have more of an appreciation for the item. Have your child observe the conversation between you and the salesperson. If you purchase online, discuss with your child what you are looking for in that purchase. If the purchase requires you to take out a loan, ask the financial counselor if they can explain to your child how they help people buy expensive items. Also have the financial counselor explain the benefit to you as the customer of their company.

Other tips for teaching your child about making big purchases are as follows:

- Explain to your child that good credit (score above 700) tells lenders you are responsible with money.
- With good credit, you are more likely to get the product or service you want with less money. You may also get a larger loan amount with a lower interest rate.

- If time permits, have the financial counselor explain to your child what good and bad credit means.
- Ask your child's opinion about the purchase and whether it is best to pay with cash or take out a loan.

Financial Trip to Favorite Restaurant

Many kids love to eat at restaurants. The combination of good food with the atmosphere of people socializing provides an excellent experience for kids. While you are in the restaurant, discuss the financial aspect with your child. Tell your child that the restaurant is a business that started with an idea. An owner is responsible for paying the servers, hosts, and cooks. The owner also purchases restaurant supplies and ingredients, including utensils, plates, tables, food, uniforms, pots, pans, etc. Explain to your child that someone owns the building in which the restaurant is located. The business owner may own the property. If not, the owner pays rent to a landlord who owns the building. The building owner does not need to be at the restaurant; they collect rent payments. The restaurant owner relies on customers to pay for supplies, employees, and rent.

Other tips for a restaurant field trip:

- Challenge your child to look around the restaurant and list other items the business owner is responsible for.
- Ask your child whether the restaurant location is good for business. Why or why not?
- If they were the business owner, what would they do differently?

- If they were the building or landowner, what would they do differently?

Financial Trip to Apartment Building

While riding around our city, I always see construction sites where they are building new apartments. This provides an excellent opportunity to discuss how apartment owners make money with your child. You may also do this with existing apartments in your area. When you see an apartment building, tell your child that the people who live there are called *tenants*. Tenants pay rent to landlords or apartment owners. Rent payments allow the tenant to live in one of the apartments. Some landlords offer extra items like a laundry room, tennis court, workout room, and pool.

Financial Trip to Meet a Business Owner

Businesses are helpful to our society because they provide products and services we need and want. They also solve our problems, improve upon existing services and ideas, and make our lives easier. In your city, town, or neighborhood, there are bound to be several entrepreneurs making our society better.

Having your child talk to business owners and interview them is a great activity. Take a trip to their place of business and find out what they do daily. Some of the questions your child can ask are as follows:

- How did you come up with this idea?
- How did you get the money to start your business?
- How many employees do you have?
- How do you find your employees?
- How do you find your customers?
- What is the best thing about being a business owner?
- What is the worst thing about being a business owner?
- Have your child create their own questions.

Bonus tip: If your child is really interested in what the business owner does, they can offer to work for the entrepreneur as an unpaid intern. This would be a valuable learning opportunity for your child. They can get the inside secrets of what it takes to be a business owner.

Field Trip to the Future

Have you ever asked a kid what they want to be when they grow up? A typical answer to this question may be a veterinarian, fireman, doctor, or astronaut. How about asking kids to share their ideas for new inventions or ways to solve problems? A child may have an idea to make their chores easier by inventing an automatic bathroom cleaner.

When a child answers these questions, why not take a field trip to the future! For the child interested in animals, schedule a field trip to the zoo and meet a zoologist. Ask your local veterinarian if your child can visit with them momentarily. Another idea is to take a nature walk and make observations about animals.

The child who wants to invent the automatic bathroom cleaner must work in smaller steps. They may begin by observing the janitor at their school. Cleaning a bathroom can be a big task, so they can start by creating an automatic toilet cleaner. The next step may be for the child to draw their invention on paper and decide what materials are needed. Afterward, take the child to a hardware store to decide on, view, and purchase the materials needed to prototype their idea.

Another way to stimulate a child's imagination is to visit the local library to read about people who share your child's interests. Having children read biographies of people who have changed our world will encourage your child to dream, invent, and be imaginative. An internet search is also beneficial to get more information about our world's innovators!

The point is to expose your child to real-life examples that match their interests! It can be fun and is a way to keep your child's brain active.

Financial Trip about Stock Market or Mutual Funds

A great way to introduce your child to the stock market is to take a field trip to a local college or university trading room. Many colleges now offer live trading rooms on campus that feature a large ticker tape and big-screen televisions broadcasting the financial news channels. Many trading rooms will also feature rows of computers and technology for analyzing stocks and companies. This real-time data and technology will introduce your child to the financial markets and the excitement of stock investing. Some colleges may even offer a virtual trading experience that students can play during their visit. Several times per year, my wife, Michelle, and I visit North Carolina A&T State University to host TRADER$: Stock Market Experience for its college students. We also facilitate the activity as a field trip for middle school students who visit the campus. This is always a fun and exciting event where we simulate one year of trading in one hour.

The Final Chapter, but Not the Final Conversation

As I sit down to write the final chapter of "Currency of Conversations," I'm reminded of our journey together. From the early chapters, where we explored the basics of budgeting and saving, to the more advanced concepts of investing and retirement planning, we've covered a lot of ground. But there's one crucial element I'd like to emphasize in this final chapter—the power of conversation.

Throughout this book, we've shared our experiences, lessons learned, and strategies for managing money effectively. But none of this knowledge is meant to be kept in isolation. It's meant to be shared and discussed with others. That's where the real magic happens.

Money isn't just about numbers and spreadsheets; it's about people and relationships. It's about the conversations we have with ourselves, our family members, friends, and even financial advisors. These conversations are the currency that can shape our financial destiny.

Think back to the analogy of the water well pump. Just as you need some water to prime the pump, you also need conversations to prime your financial journey. Conversations with trusted friends and family members can support and encourage you to start saving, investing, and building your wealth. Through these conversations, you can share your goals, dreams, and fears and receive valuable insights and advice.

But it's not just about talking; it's also about listening. Listening to the experiences and perspectives of others can broaden your horizons and help you make more informed financial decisions.

It's about seeking out mentors and experts who can guide you on your path to financial success.

So, my call to action for you is simple—start having more conversations about money. Break the taboo that often surrounds financial matters. Discuss your financial goals with your partner, children, and friends. Share your successes and your challenges. Seek out financial communities and support groups where you can learn from others and offer your insights in return.

In the digital age, countless forums, blogs, and social media groups are dedicated to personal finance. Join them, participate actively, and build a network of like-minded individuals who can help you on your journey. Engage with financial experts and seek their guidance when needed.

But remember, the most important conversation you'll ever have is with yourself. It's the internal dialogue where you confront your beliefs, fears, and desires regarding money. It's where you set your financial goals and commit to achieving them. It's where you constantly evaluate your progress and make adjustments.

As we conclude our journey together through "Currency of Conversations," I want you to carry this message: Money is not just about dollars and cents; it's about the conversations surrounding it. Embrace these conversations, share your knowledge, and seek wisdom from others. Together, we can create a world where financial literacy is accessible, and everyone can achieve their financial goals.

Thank you for joining me on this adventure. I believe in your ability to take control of your financial destiny, and I'm excited to see the positive impact you'll have on your life and those around you. Remember, the currency of conversation is a powerful tool—use it wisely, and you'll be amazed at the wealth it can generate, not just in your bank account but in your life.

Now, go out there and start those conversations. Your financial future awaits, and you have the knowledge and tools to shape it as you see fit.

"Let me put it simply: I've got more disposable income than many others, and it's all thanks to Linsey Mills, my financial consultant. I've been living within my means for a significant amount of time, and now I'm reaping the rewards."

~Loyal Client Over 20 Years